STAYING AHEAD AT WORK

A selection of other How To Books

Achieving Personal Well-being
Applying for a Job
Building Self-Esteem
Career Networking
Career Planning for Women
Communicate at Work
Conducting Effective Interviews
Conducting Effective Negotiations
Finding a Job with a Future
Getting That Job
Investing in People
Know Your Rights at Work
Learning New Job Skills
Making Decisions
Making Effective Speeches
Manage an Office

Manage Your Career
Managing Meetings
Managing Projects
Managing Successful Teams
Managing Through People
Managing Your Time
Managing Yourself
Market Yourself
Organising Effective Training
Self-Counselling
Starting a New Career
Starting to Manage
Unlocking Your Potential
Winning Presentations
Writing a CV that Works
Writing a Report

Other titles in preparation

The How To series now contains more than 200 titles in the following categories:

Business & Management
Computer Basics
General Reference
Jobs & Careers
Living & Working Abroad

Personal Finance
Self-Development
Small Business
Student Handbooks
Successful Writing

Please send for a free copy of the latest catalogue for full details (see back cover for address).

JOBS & CAREERS

STAYING AHEAD AT WORK

How to develop a winning portfolio
of work skills and attitudes

Karen Mannering

How To Books

Cartoons by Mike Flanagan

British Library Cataloguing in Publication Data
A catalogue record for this book is available from the British Library.

© Copyright 1998 by Karen Mannering.

First published in 1998 by How To Books Ltd, 3 Newtec Place,
Magdalen Road, Oxford, OX4 1RE, United Kingdom.
Tel: (01865) 793806. Fax: (01865) 248780.

Note: The material contained in this book is set out in good faith for
general guidance and no liability can be accepted for loss or expense
incurred as a result of relying in particular circumstances on statements
made in this book. The law and regulations may be complex and liable to
change, and readers should check the current position with the relevant
authorities before making personal arrangements.

Produced for How To Books by Deer Park Productions.
Typeset by Concept Communications (Design & Print) Ltd, Crayford, Kent.
Printed and bound by Cromwell Press, Trowbridge, Wiltshire.

Contents

List of Illustrations

*Mind Map® is the registered trade mark of the Buzan Organisation used with permission.

Preface

The contract between worker and employer is changing. No longer is an employer able to guarantee a job, or even a career, for life. Neither should an employee wed themselves to an organisation for the promise of security – for it will not be there. If we are to survive we have to change too. It is no longer enough to sit tight and hope that somehow, if we keep quiet, we will be overlooked when the hammer that is redundancy, strikes. It is a jungle out there and it is the survival of the fittest.

The rules have changed too. Qualifications alone will no longer guarantee promotion. Instead you will be judged on your ability to resolve conflict, negotiate a fair contract, motivate people to work for you, and demonstrate commitment towards your future development. Getting ahead will be tough and staying ahead, tougher still.

This book will show you ways in which you can kick-start both your personal and professional development needs. Using exercises designed to carry you forward, you will identify your skills and learn which of these require further development. Throughout the book you will be building up your own portfolio of skills, which can then be maintained as a personal reference, shared with your manager, or presented at an interview. The exercises and suggestions throughout can either serve as discussion points or as a personal workbook. It is up to you.

It is your future, it is your career, it is your choice.

ACKNOWLEDGEMENTS

In writing this book I would like to acknowledge the following for their unerring help and support. Giles Lewis and Nikki Read who provided the opportunity. Derek, my husband who provided the space for me to write. And finally, Richard Hemmings, Adrian Greenwood, Richard Hicks and Emma Pavitt – a team *par excellence* without whom this book would never have been written.

Karen Mannering

1
Visiting the Future

Change is a great dilemma – most of us enjoy new experiences, but stability is the bedrock on which a great deal of our comfort, well-being and happiness is founded. No matter what your view of change, one thing is certain: change is the future. We must all adapt to change, or the future will be very bleak indeed.

SEEING INTO THE FUTURE

How nice it would be to be able to gaze into the future – to see what will happen and then make any necessary adaptations. Unfortunately crystal balls are not that reliable, but there are a number of maxims and good advice to guide us. Management 'gurus' are telling us that the way we work in the future will be different and to be forewarned is to be forearmed.

Forearming ourselves adequately will provide us with an insurance policy against the uncertainties of the future. Evolution involves the adaptation and survival of the fittest. The goal of this book is to help you to evolve to survive. After all, it is far better to ride on the crest of the wave in this ever evolving world than to be lost in its wake.

The business world is changing and that will be reflected in the way that people work in the future. So many industries have disappeared, and careers vanished. There is now no such thing as a comptomator operator or typing pool supervisors. Some people are being made redundant because they failed to keep pace with the need for updated and different skills. Feeling secure in jobs they thought would last forever, they never saw the need to branch out or extend their experiences.

Seeing which way the wind blows
There is no crystal ball that will show us the world of work in the future, but we can make predictions in several ways:

● listening to management 'gurus'

- observing the big companies, what are they doing? Where are they placing their resources?

- which sectors are doing well/failing?

- looking out for up and coming innovations and trends.

As with all predictions there is a certain amount of guesswork and assumptions. In reality jobs and employment have always changed and evolved, but at a much slower pace. It is the speed of today's changes which is alarming. It seems that one moment you are the new whizz-kid and, a few years later, yesterday's news.

TRANSLATING THIS INTO REALITY

Companies are changing. Headquarters are slimming down to a smaller number of key staff responsible for managing, co-ordinating and monitoring the whole operation. Staff will be bought in as and when their skills are needed.

There are no longer 'jobs for life'. In some cases career paths have been cut short, often by the introduction of new technology. The success of telephone banking, for which staff have telephone and computer skills, has had a dramatic effect on those who had a career path in high street banking. Even in local government and the civil service, dramatic changes to organisational structures have led to high levels of redundancies with many senior 'white-collar' staff leaving with no job prospects. A situation unheard of ten years ago.

It is not unusual today to find people taking retirement packages whilst still in their early 50s. They often then branch out into another career or take on some part-time work.

Technology now allows more people to work from home. There is no longer the need for many employees to be sited in the office, all day, every day. This will have a profound effect on home life and our perceptions of 'going to work'.

IDENTIFYING THE NEW SKILLS WE WILL NEED

In the past it was always those who were good at a technical task who rose to the role of manager. The logic behind this was that if you were good at a task then you were in a position to monitor others' performance of the same task. It also formed part of a reward system and workers rose through the ranks during their career. This process did not recognise that managing people needs different skills. The result was a workforce of managers (with poor people skills) who were highly competent workers (but weren't doing that work).

Employers of the future will be looking for a new type of workforce to work in a new way. People who have generic and transferable skills will be more valuable as they can be deployed to do many differing tasks. For example, project management skills will ensure that the person could manage and monitor any project, regardless of the subject matter. This would give them a wide scope for employability within an organisation which works in project management style.

In the future people skills will be more highly rewarded. The ability to encourage staff to work with you and give 100 per cent will be more valued than being able to operate equipment or machinery. Maintaining motivation in your staff will be ranked higher than completing progress reports. Communication skills at all levels will be of the highest importance – sending out the right messages, in the right way, at the right time. Something that was once a management/media skill is now invaluable for everyone.

A great deal of team work will be evident in this new working life. Teams will exist to work on projects, and teams will be pulled together to tackle difficult problems. People may find themselves brought into a team to fulfil a specialist role, or their skills may form part of the variety of skills required to obtain the optimum team composition. High performance teams are not made up of six or eight of the same type of people: each person should be selected for the contribution they can make to the team. The ability to work with others and recognise everyone's strengths will be paramount, as will the knowledge of effective team formation and management.

FEELING THE BENEFITS

It is important to recognise the benefits of working in this new way. There will be more choice in the number and types of organisations you can work for. There will be greater financial recognition for those who have the skills to adapt to the new patterns of working. Each individual will have responsibility for their own learning and development and control over the way in which their career progresses.

Health warning
Developing yourself could severely enhance your career prospects but it is a road of no return. Prepare well in advance, discovery can be addictive!

Consider the advantages and disadvantages of this new way of working as listed below:

Advantages

You take control of your own career destiny.

You will have a range of contacts to tap into.

The type and breadth of work you can do is extended.

Disadvantages

You may feel insecure at first.

It takes time.

You will have to undergo some self analysis.

All of the disadvantages can be overcome through planning and careful consideration.

- **Insecurity** can be countered by the number and quality of contacts with which you interact. It can also be remedied by ensuring you are clear about the range of skills you possess and how you intend to market and present them.

- **Learning** takes time. You would not expect to learn a foreign language to any great standard in a week. However, by starting now you will be one step ahead of others.

- **Self analysis** can be both joyous and painful. Finding that we do not have an aptitude for a certain skill can be difficult to accept; however, if the individual is willing there is often a compromise situation.

For example, Colin considered himself an excellent manager. He completed all reports on time and charted the team's leave and sickness. No one could question his organisational abilities. When he asked them for feedback, his team, however, found his communications skills lacking. He appeared to show little interest in their personal development and just sent them on statutory training courses. Colin found it difficult to understand the new and different approach to management needed by his team. The team wanted a leader who cared about them, not someone doing a time and motion study. Luckily Colin found out in time and worked on his softer 'people skills' and won back the confidence of his team.

PREPARING FOR THIS NEW WAY OF WORKING

Mental preparation is crucial. The world around us is changing and we will have to change to adapt to it. Acceptance of change is the first step towards surmounting the challenge it poses. Time spent thinking about ourselves, our jobs, our lives, is time invested in our future.

In a volatile situation such as a re-organisation, think about how much time and effort you can spend on hanging on to the job you have – just treading water. If you put as much effort into developing yourself, you will succeed in not only 'hanging in there' but climbing higher too.

> **Remember, in any volatile situation there are winners and losers. Just make sure you are one of the winners.**

CASE STUDIES

The following case studies are of fictitious people at various stages of their careers. At the end of each chapter, their progress will be documented, choosing and using the exercises shown within the chapter to demonstrate their progress.

Richard feels threatened

Richard is 45, married and has a family. He has worked in local government since he was 21 and is now a group manager. He has a degree in English. He has no further qualifications, although he has attended many training courses throughout his career. He joined local government because it offered him a career structure and stability, a factor which became more important as he married, bought a house, and had a family. Richard's wife, Elaine, has never worked and therefore he is the main breadwinner. His two children are now at university and he has to contribute financial support. Richard feels threatened by the uncertainty of the future. His job is increasingly being re-evaluated, and he sees his colleagues leaving. He had hoped that he would have many years left to work but feels that no one values his experience. He sees younger people being offered the opportunities that exist and colleagues in their 50s being pensioned off.

Carol returns to work

Carol is 36 and has returned to work after having three children. Now she has made the decision to return, she has discovered ambition and is keen to climb the career ladder. She is working as clerical support in the personnel department of the Northern Bank. Before having children,

Carol worked as a typist/receptionist for a building firm. She has no qualifications and is worried about how the working environment has changed. She is not used to working in such a competitive team, but is determined that hard work and a dedication to the tasks will help to get her noticed.

Dean has been working for one year

Dean is 23 and left university with a BSc in Computing Studies. He took six months off thinking that, when he chose to start work, the world would be his oyster. He has up-to-date computer skills but did not find getting a job as easy as he expected. He has had to take a job in a small sized computer company, at a lower salary than he would have liked. He has returned to live at home but would like a place of his own which he could share with his girlfriend, Sarah. She has started working in a travel agents as a trainee, but also has a low income. Dean is learning that technical skills are not the only criteria employers look for in recruiting people for top jobs, but he is not sure where to start, as they taught him nothing about this at university.

POINTS TO CONSIDER

1. If your organisation is in the process of a major change, write down four other jobs you could do.

2. Think about the worst thing (work related) that could be exposed about you (*eg* poor timekeeping, consistently leaves early, hands in poor quality work) – be honest!

3. Now consider how you could counter both the problem and deal with the embarrassment of being confronted with it.

2
Preparing Yourself

As with all great journeys it pays to spend some time in preparation. Self development is not handed out on a plate, or given as some reward. It is *your* personal development that you wish to undertake to give you the edge over others. It is only right, therefore, that you think carefully about the level of your commitment. Remember, some people dream of success . . . while others work hard at attaining it.

DEVELOPING THE RIGHT ATTITUDE TOWARDS LEARNING

So what is an attitude, and why is one right and another not?

People often comment that someone has a good or bad attitude to something. What they are talking about is someone's tendency to behave in one way rather than another. One point to remember is that statements about attitude are always subjective. The person judging that attitude is comparing it with their own perception of acceptable behaviour in the situation. However, because of the way in which our society has formed, some common images emerge. These are the rules that masquerade as 'manners'. Practise good manners as they will endear you to the people who can help you move upwards. They are also essential in the new business environment where forming quick relationships and effective communication play such major roles.

Developing an attitude for learning

Think for one moment. If you needed to develop a positive attitude towards learning what would this entail?

1. An open or enquiring mind?

2. Setting some spare time aside?

3. Budgeting a percentage of your salary as a financial investment in your future?

These are just three suggestions; I am sure you can think of many others.

You only learn if you want to.

This may seem an obvious statement, but the truth is that no one can force you to learn. For example, you will only read onwards in this book if you can see the benefit of doing so (this is the 'pay-back' principle). In every action we do there has to be something in it for us, to carry that action through.

Some benefits of self development
Think of some of the benefits of making your future development an integral part of your every day life:

● seeing your career take-off

● acquiring distinct advantages over others in career advancement

● gaining new and marketable skills

● maintaining employability

● improving mental agility

● making contacts through effective networking

● enlarging networks to include senior and influential colleagues.

If these prospects excite you then you have just the right attitude towards your own development. Read on to find out how these can be put into action.

MOTIVATING YOURSELF

Procrastination, it has been said, is the grave in which opportunity is buried. Why struggle to do today what can be done tomorrow?

The answer is, of course, that while you are thinking about it someone else has been there, done it, and is already ahead. Personal motivation is inextricably linked to your perception of what you will be getting out of this input of time and energy. In other words the 'pay-back' principle again.

Many people think that they go to work only for money, but his has been proved time and time again not to be true. Of course earning money is an important factor, but there are others. At work we meet with groups of friends, communicate and take part in the kind of social interaction that we may not encounter in the home environment.

Spend five minutes thinking about what would motivate you in the following situations:

● getting up earlier for work

● staying late to finish that special report

● going out on a cold, dark night to attend an exercise class.

Is it the money? How about the praise and recognition? Or the pride of overcoming or controlling negative feelings? It could be that your motivation is different in each case.

Why is it important to know?

Being able to analyse the reason for your motivation is important. It is by identifying and acknowledging your motivating factors that you will be able to apply them to difficult situations, and sail through. For example, if you are struggling to construct a difficult proposal, take a moment to think about how you felt when you completed that other highly complex piece of work last month.

Experience again the frustration of wrestling with the workload against the clock? What made you carry on?

Now think of how you felt when it was all over and the job was complete. Were you complimented on your work? Re-live the warm glow of satisfaction you felt for a job well done. Feel the positive energy flowing through you.

Use the same motivation to carry you through again. You were successful last time, therefore you will be again . . . You can achieve anything!

Congratulations, you have just given your motivation another injection of power to help you continue.

Personal motivation is selfish. No other person can supply you with reasons to fuel your motivation. You need to identify your own motivating factors.

> **Remember – this career development is for you and not for someone else.**

FINDING HELP

Help is all around, you just have to know how to tap into it. Start by auditing your organisation. What can they offer in the way of help with your development? Find out whether they have a self development library or any packages, tapes, *etc* covering management techniques that you could borrow for a short time. If they don't then visit your local library, as most now stock a selection of these materials, or have access to them. Find out too whether your organisation has set up support networks, special interest groups or mentoring/coaching schemes.

In addition to the practical side, you also need to find out your organisation's attitude to learning. Do they profess to be a learning organisation or do they feel that any non-job related development should be the responsibility of the individual? It is important that you find out the corporate culture towards development as it will influence how you approach your development action plan (see Chapter 3) and the choice of options open to you.

Using the organisation
Find out if help is available from within the organisation:

- Is there an in-house development scheme or career advice available?

- Is there a separate training department or is it covered by personnel?

- Is there a mentoring or coaching scheme?

In addition ask your manager about how the training budget for the department is allocated? Can the budget be used outside the organisation or only on internal schemes and programmes?

Using professional institutions
Most jobs can be allied to a particular professional group or sub-group. You may or may not be a member of one of these institutes, but in addition to the range of services they provide, they usually produce a magazine or journal, hold seminars and regional meetings. These are all fodder for anyone serious about their development. The journals usually cover interesting career profiles and focus on aspects of the job in detail. They regularly feature new research and review new books. All this is in addition to the credibility afforded to you as a member of an institute.

Note that if you want to move away from your current career, you shouldn't invest more time and resources in gaining full membership of an institute covering your current job. It would be wiser to concentrate on becoming an associate or affiliated member of an institute which covers your chosen field.

Using continuous professional development (CPD) groups

Finding others with the same ideas on self development can be very supportive in the first instance. Many professional institutes have Continuous Professional Development (CPD) groups where people meet who want to share their learning experiences with others and also benefit from the interaction of discussions within the group. At these groups, members raise their interest in pursuing development in certain subject areas and request the help of the group in progressing that development.

Using your local authority

Most local authorities will be able to provide you with some level of career advice through either adult career advice centres, or their education departments. One very good reason for searching out these helpful resources is that they have access to psychometric tests which enable the user to find out what career area is more suited to their temperament, personality and strengths. Although the results from these tests should only be used as a guide, they can highlight a certain flair in a particular area, and will recommend a selection of possible careers, some of which may not be obvious.

Using colleges and universities

Colleges and universities are a helpful resource when you know where you are intending to take your development. However, most offer limited advice to those who want to explore several different career avenues. Also as their qualifications are divided into departments, for example, 'Education' or 'Information Technology', it can be quite difficult to find information on a career which crosses several departments – for example, becoming a computer trainer.

MAKING THE FIRST MOVES

At this stage you are only putting out feelers and considering what advice may be available.

Explore your organisation or company in the first instance. Locate the personnel or training department and make an appointment with someone who is available to talk about career prospects. As part of your preparation, check their position on the department's organisational chart, or consult others to ensure you are talking to the right person.

If you work in a smaller company you may not have access to this level of information. Start by discussing your development with a manager or senior colleague. If this would not be prudent, then seek some independent advice through an adult careers centre, or identify a person in another company who has the role you covet and think about approaching them for information.

INTEGRATING REGULAR TRAINING

Your company or organisation probably has some form of regular training schedule or prospectus. Sometimes this training is provided in-house and in other cases it may be handled by an external organisation. Wherever possible look to integrate any regular training you receive into your personal plan for development.

Below are some advantages and disadvantages to company training you may like to think about:

Advantages	Disadvantages
It is funded by the company.	You have little control over content.
It is usually in company time.	It may not, at first sight, seem to progress your career aspirations.
It allows you to network with other members of the company you may otherwise never meet.	It may not offer any recognised qualification.

In some instances the training will be so generic, for example 'customer care', that it is useful in any job. In others it will be specific to your job, but you may be able to pull out of it some more cross-border learning points.

For example, imagine you have been sent on a one day course to learn about a computer presentation package which you will need in your job as secretary to produce presentation material and overheads. It may seem that this training is purely job specific and does not further your career aspirations. However, during your training course you will be able to re-cap on your knowledge of the computer operating system. You will also learn valuable lessons about how a presentation should be phased, and how to convey information with greater impact.

These are valuable lessons which are **transportable skills**. Such skills are there in every training course, you just have to look for them.

Being proactive

Find a copy of your organisation's training schedule and note:

- the courses which are designed to increase effectiveness in your current job

- the courses which you feel could benefit your future career.

Which courses fulfil both sets of criteria? These are the courses to target in the first instance because they benefit both your career future and your current job and should be fully funded. Make a note of them and keep them at hand – you can add them to your portfolio later (see Chapter 5).

Being reactive

If your training is solely determined by your manager or by organisational restraints, do not worry. In your portfolio, make a note of the courses or training you are due to undertake. Now harness some lateral thinking. Try to extract other benefits which *you* could gain from the training. You need to do this exercise before undertaking the training. This is so that when you are undertaking the training you can actively seek out opportunities which meet *your* objectives in addition to those of the company, and be in a position to exploit them.

CASE STUDIES

Richard gets moving

Richard has a degree which he achieved 21 years ago. Although a degree always has currency Richard needs to demonstrate that he used his degree as a first step towards his professional development. He needs to tie up all the training he has had over the years to prove that he has a range of skills which he has maintained and used during his working life. He needs to show that he has built on those skills and learnt new ones, demonstrating his commitment to progressing his career development. He starts by listing all the training courses he can remember attending.

Carol takes a closer look at the Northern Bank

When Carol went to work at the Northern Bank it just seemed like a reasonable job. However, now Carol has decided to take a closer interest in her career, she decides to find out what the Northern Bank can do for her. Carol remembers that during the induction programme they were all told about the company training plan. She gets out her notes again and phones the personnel department to find out more about it. The plan sounds promising and so Carol makes a note in her diary to raise the issue of training at her next progress meeting with her manager.

Dean checks out his attitude

Dean has experienced a number of knocks. He did not receive many job offers when he decided to start work, and then he did not get the level of job he thought he should have been offered. He is starting to realise that climbing the career ladder is not as easy as he thought. He thinks hard about his time at university. Although it was hard work, his spare time was his own. It did not matter how he dressed or presented himself. Now Dean realises that he has been catapulted into a working situation where it takes effort to move ahead. Putting more effort into his self development may mean spending less time watching television, being with his mates, or talking to Sarah. Is it worth it? Only Dean can answer this, but he knows that if he is to go down this path he is going to have to change his attitude.

POINTS TO CONSIDER

1.   Ask yourself whether you have the right attitude towards learning. Are you prepared to give up some of your leisure time to further your career (short term pain for long term gain)?

2.   Find out your organisation's attitude towards training. Are they a 'learning organisation' or do they provide training on a need only basis?

3.   Contact your local library and ask whether they have a list or prospectus of the learning materials they have on offer.

3
Developing a Toolkit

To succeed as a key member of an organisation it is vital that you deploy an appropriate range of skills. The aim of this chapter is to provide you with the necessary tools to undertake an audit of your skills in relation to increasing your value at work and building your skills portfolio (your toolkit for success).

Figure 1 is a skills audit route map which presents the tools in their logical running order. It will enable you to see where these tools fit into the process. For example, the route map starts with a personal skills audit which involves identifying the technical skills and soft skills you possess. The next phase is to consider life experiences . . . and so on.

Complete the tasks outlined in the sections that follow and you will be taking the first steps in securing your future. There will be exercises to complete which will be compiled into a portfolio at a later stage (Chapter 5).

PERFORMING A PERSONAL SKILLS AUDIT

A personal skills audit will help you learn more about yourself and the time you spend undertaking this audit will be an investment in your future. You should know your capabilities and strengths better than anyone, but when do you ever have time to lay out your full range of skills, perhaps in relation to the jobs you have done in the past, and analyse it to see if patterns emerge? Undertaking the skills audit does take time, but it can be an enlightening experience from which you can plan your future.

The different skills we possess can be divided into technical skills, soft skills, and experiential skills (see Using Life Experiences below).

Technical skills
Technical skills are action-based skills, for example, word processing or driving a car. It is quite likely that you have received some kind of training to be able to perform these skills. They are skills that are easily

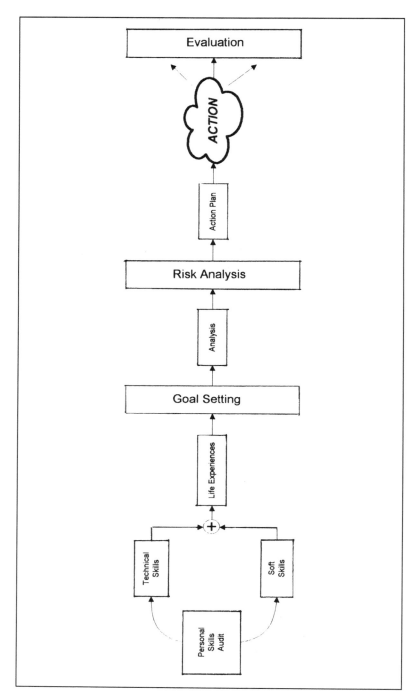

Fig. 1. Skills audit route map.

identifiable and tested. They are the practical skills that, in many occupations, get a job done.

Soft skills

Soft skills are harder to identify. They are the emotional and mental skills which make one person, for example, a better communicator than another. Some more examples of soft skills are:

● effective listening

● negotiating

● reasoning

● nurturing

● analytical thought.

These skills contribute to make us more effective in our working life. They are intangible and therefore are more difficult to test than technical skills. However, we all possess a range of soft skills, and it is these soft skills as much as technical skills that employers are looking for today and in the future.

When should I start my skills audit?

Now! The sooner you start the better. Just follow the route map and undertake each section in this chapter. This is your first step towards a greater investment in your future.

Starting the skills audit

Forget your job title, instead consider the type of work you have been doing during your career. Consider:

● whether you worked in a team or alone

● the type of employer you had (private sector or local government)

● the management structure

● the skills you used (both technical and soft skills).

Think about each of your jobs, one at a time, and on a sheet of paper divided lengthways into two columns do the following:

1. In the left hand column, write down what you liked about the job (try to think in terms of skills you enjoyed using or were good at).

2. In the right hand column, write down what you disliked about the job (again try to express yourself in skills).

3. Fold the paper so that you can no longer see what you have written, and repeat steps one and two for the next job, and so on until you have finished your list of jobs. (Don't worry if you prefer to express yourself in sentences, for example, 'I enjoyed co-ordinating the Reps diaries when they phoned into the office'. At a later point these will be gathered together into skills groups.)

4. Add to the list any other skills you are good at, or people have commented on.

See Figure 2 for an example.

Keep the piece of paper in a drawer or, if you are bold, pin it on your notice board. Don't rush ahead – you will need to reflect on your list over the following few days to build up a stronger picture. Believe it or not this rest or incubation period is an essential part of generating and/or developing ideas.

USING LIFE EXPERIENCES

Most people have encountered life experiences that form how we think and feel. These could be from situations which have occurred at work, at home, or during a hobby/pastime. They are situations which generate personal growth. Correlations can often be made from these situations into work situations enabling you to handle them more effectively.

Of the three types of skill (technical, soft and experiential), experiential skills can be the most contentious. It may be argued that these skills are not always transferable. Many women believe that running a team is easy compared with bringing up three small children on a tight budget, and that many of the management skills required are the same. However, not everyone would accept this alone as a measure of competence. What would be accepted is that success in these areas demonstrates a flair in the individual for management, and therefore they form the basis for further study (or training) into management skills.

Some demonstration of courage within your life should also form part of your audit. It could be some act of outward bravery or inward, emotional courage. Dealing with a serious illness in either yourself or a

I liked	_I disliked_

Barkers Manufacturers

team atmosphere	too much noise
team meetings	entering statistics all day
telephone contact	

Duchess Tea Rooms

helping people	difficult customers
making people happy	cleaning up
	adding up in my head

Legal Eagle Ltd

organising my own workload	copy typing
friendly staff	difficult, demanding bosses
using latest technology	filing
taking calls and dealing with the	strict working hours
public	no promotional prospects

Completely Computer

working on my own initiative	calculations
good team spirit	invoice work
flexible working patterns	no staff room or restaurant
ringing other offices for information	customer complaints
organising team events	

Fig. 2. A sample job skills audit.

loved one is very stressful and shows fortitude and strength. Try not to look at the actual event but concentrate on the outcome. What can you learn about yourself from the experience?

Integrating voluntary work

Voluntary work can cover all activities from serving free dinners to the elderly to serving in charity shops. Even helping out at a school fete or sports day can be considered voluntary work. What is common to all of these is that you are working, using skills which can be recognised. Most voluntary groups today are very professional in their approach. There are opportunities to attend or speak at meetings. You might also have to chair some of them. All this is valuable experience and you may wish to reflect on which part of the job you like most and those you like least.

Appreciating travel experiences

Someone once said that travel broadens the mind. It certainly gives us an insight into different cultures and ways of life. This type of knowledge is becoming more important as companies assume international status. The world is getting much smaller and 'international managing' is emerging as a distinct skill in itself. Even if you did not learn the language of the countries you visited, a knowledge of how their differing cultures approach business (and life) is very valuable to an organisation which wants to trade in the international market. Experiencing cultures in other countries enables us to question how our own culture works, and whether we think it is right. This questioning is valuable in developing the kind of enquiring mind needed for innovators.

> **Life experiences enable us to grow as people. These skills give us depth and variety and are unique to each of us.**

Questions to ask yourself

1. Have you ever travelled extensively or experienced the culture of other countries?

2. Do you have a pastime or hobby which brings you into contact with a large diversity of people?

3. Have you ever experienced a situation which has made you question your fundamental beliefs on life?

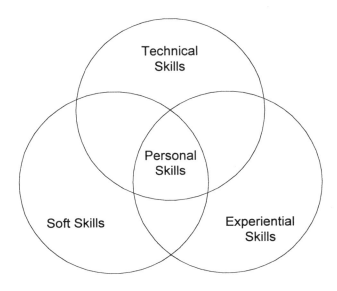

Fig. 3. The relationship between skills.

Remember – all life experiences are very important and shape us as individuals.

SETTING GOALS

Effective **goal setting** will be an important part of your toolkit. You would not embark on a long journey without knowing where you are going and assessing progress on route. It is the same with your career. Setting goals allows you to set out your future in manageable steps which have been pre-planned. They are marker posts for completing each stage. They also give you permission to celebrate your success. Did I say 'celebrate'? Yes indeed, celebration of your success in meeting and exceeding goals is a very important part of building self-esteem.

The most common reason for people not setting goals is that they are afraid of the risk of not meeting them. They fear that they will appear to have failed. This is absolutely wrong and in no way should goals ever become sticks to be beaten with. They are merely aids in helping the mind to focus on several key achievements which lead to the overall aim. It is not unusual for goals to change periodically. It could be that:

● they have been achieved and therefore new goals are required

● they need to be targeted again more precisely

● they are no longer relevant.

Sometimes a new opportunity arises at work and work veers off at a tangent, leaving your goals looking inappropriate and out of date. For this reason, although goals may be set annually, they should be revisited quarterly to ensure they are still valid.

Setting goals seems easy until you start. Do you set goals that are long distance, for example, 'To be Managing Director' or do you go in at a much lower level, 'To survive until payday!'? To help, think of the following three levels as being like building blocks:

● your purpose

● your aim

● your goals.

Defining your purpose

This is your *raison d'être,* your reason for being. Everyone at some time feels an innate sense of living for a purpose and some people are able to weave this into their working life. Very talented business people volunteer to work, unpaid, to help charities develop their business. They often do this because, outside the push and shove of big business, it gives purpose to their lives. They believe they are helping someone more needy and it may be a particular charity with which they have an affinity. They may set goals within this work but their *purpose* for undertaking the work is not a goal. There are no time barriers on your purpose as it is a journey that lasts a lifetime.

Establishing your aim

Your **aim** will be your top level goal, so it may be the title of the job you covet. It is helpful to give it a time restriction, which you can always adjust. An example of an aim is:

'To be a training manager within a blue chip organisation by the time I am 40 years old.'

Of course the more specific the goal, the better for focusing the mind. If you know the name of the company you want to work for, then state it. You could even add the salary. Your aim gives you an overall framework of where you want to go and your goals *must* relate to this aim.

Setting your goals

These will be short sentences which support your aim. In effect they provide milestones to ensure that you are going in the right direction. Try to keep them specific and sharp, vague references are of little help and can be misconstrued at a later date; for example, don't say,

'To increase profits by 15 per cent'.

This is far too vague: 15 per cent from what? Which part of the business is included in this? When should this effect be felt? In one year, two? When you come back to re-visit this goal later, will you even remember the initial profit figures to confirm that you have increased by 15 per cent? Instead try,

'To increase profits from £100,000 to £115,000 within the next twelve months through the implementation of the marketing plan.'

This may be more wordy but it is precise and focused with actual figures, a set time limit and a method of achievement.

Try to pinpoint an overall aim for your career and then write between three and six goals which support that aim. Write them somewhere prominent and try to look at them every day.

Recognising organisational goals

You may find that within your organisation's appraisal system there is an opportunity to pinpoint a number of goals for the following year. These goals will be specific to your job and will reflect the overall business aims of the organisation. They are unlikely to be the same as *your personal goals* for planning *your future*. You may find that the goals which are acceptable within the appraisal system do not leave sufficient room for personal career growth or movement, and this is why it is important to undertake this exercise using your personal career plans, outside the organisation.

Celebrating your successes

On a new piece of paper write the heading, 'My Successes'. Now start a list of the major successes you have had throughout your life. Every time you experience another triumph in your life, add it to the list. It is so important to applaud our successes, however small they may be. When you are next faced with a difficult project or decision to make, take a look at that page. Read down the list and feel the strength swelling up inside you as you experience, once again, previous projects and situations which you successfully completed and won. Now think once again about that difficult project or decision. There should be no question in your mind that you can succeed – after all you have succeeded in so many other things, where could you go wrong?

> **Re-living or celebrating success is important in shaping attitude and developing a positive approach to tasks.**

On another new page write out 'Success means . . ' about six times, down the left hand side of the page. When you have finished, complete the sentences writing down what success means to you, for example:

'Success means managing the department', or
'Success means owning a new car every year'.

The purpose of this exercise is that *you* define *your* criteria for success. Success means different things to different people, but the only person your success really matters to is you, so it makes sense that you set the rules. The results will be far more powerful than any success criteria imposed on you from others, and in the process you will learn more about yourself and where you should be going to experience personal success.

ANALYSING YOUR SKILLS AUDIT

You are now ready to start analysing your skills audit. To do this you will have to take an holistic approach to your data. It is similar to a fortune teller reading the cards, you will have to group and make sense of all the information collected rather than take each one on its own.

Starting with your dislikes

Look back at the lists of skills compiled from your previous jobs. Firstly concentrate on the column in which you listed the parts of the jobs you did not like. We will make the assumption that as you did not like those parts of the job, it is probable that you are not so strong in those skills areas as we tend to like what we do well. Look at your list and think of the situations you described: can you pinpoint more precisely which aspect of them you felt uncomfortable with? For example, you may have written: 'Hated monthly meetings with sales team'. This could be for any of the following reasons:

●   you had to chair those meetings and did not feel in control (chairing meeting skills)

● you had to arrange the meetings and did not enjoy that organisational aspect of your job (organisational skills)

● you always felt you had little to offer in the way of participation in the meetings (team participation skills)

● the meeting was always held too early in the morning for you (communication, negotiating, and time management skills)

● you disliked a particular member of the team (skills in handling conflict)

● the meeting always resulted in a large amount of work for you afterwards (time management and organisational skills).

All of these are plausible but you will need to analyse each of *your* points in turn to place the dislikes into skills language.

On the following page, you will find a list of skills which will help you express the points you have written, in skill terminology. Using a red pen, write the skills you can identify beside each of your examples, so that they stand out. Once this is completed, look down the list. It is possible that a repeating pattern or trend may emerge.

These results will be either:

● indicators of where development is required, or

● definitions of job functions you want to avoid.

These are your negative skills areas.

Looking at your strengths

Now look at the column down which you listed the skills or the things you liked doing. We will assume that, because you enjoyed that part of your job, you felt a high level of confidence. In turn this confidence comes from the fact that you probably perform well in these skills areas – these are you positive skills.

As in the previous section try to analyse the situation so that you extract the particular skill in which you excelled. This is no time to be shy, if you were good at something then say so! Again write each skill name in red pen on your list.

Analysing your life experiences

You will need to repeat the previous exercise again with your life expe-

List of possible skills

information gathering	creativity	visualisation
new ideas	developing ideas	organisation
diagnosing	analysing	categorising
predicting	forecasting	budgeting
objective setting	targeting	decision making
facilitating	exploring	questioning
assessing	interpreting	exploring
expanding ideas	dexterity	planning
communicating	negotiating	co-ordinating
motivating	persuading	initiating
enthusing others	interpreting data	calculating
speaking	presenting	risk taking
instructing	teaching	training
prioritising	time management	resourcing
encouraging	caring/nurturing	listening
researching	counselling	coaching
pacing	measuring	comparing
observing	pinpointing detail	being strategic
reviewing	concluding	adapting

riences only this time a little more integration is required. Each time you identify a skill or development area, look back at your positive and negative skills. Does the data tie together?

You are looking for links between your identified strong skills (positive skills) or development needs (negative skills), and those in your life experiences. For example, in your left hand column showing positive skills (what you liked about your jobs) you may have written, 'Liked being responsible for two younger members of the team'. You may have written 'caring' or 'nurturing' skills, in red, beside this. When overlaying your life experiences you may find one of your accomplishments was raising a family, or looking after a relative in their old age – demonstrating reinforcement of your caring skills.

Work down your list, tying in as many strong skills and development areas as possible. Underline any positive skills which are reinforced through your life experiences.

Tying-in your goals

Place your list of goals alongside your skills audit. Read through them objectively and for each one ask yourself whether you have the range of strong skills to accomplish each goal, using your audit. Look down the column listing your development areas (your negative skills). Are there any development areas which would obstruct you reaching your goal? For example if your goal is

'To be an accountant in the next five years'

then a negative area in mathematics or calculations would require a considerable amount of development if the goal is ever to be achieved. Although significant improvements in skills may be achieved, you need to be realistic and take into consideration the time and commitment required.

If you identify the need for a skill in which you are not strong or do not like, then there are only two courses of action. Either:

1. **Change the goal** – parameters may need to be softened. For example if your mathematics and statistics are not so hot, you may decide it more prudent to become a budget manager rather than an accountant.

2. **Develop the skill** – which may have time and resource implications. For example if you wanted to make a career change into the legal profession, you would need to be prepared to step right back to the beginning; and legal training can be expensive. These are difficult choices and each individual may take a different decision.

DEVELOPING A RISK ANALYSIS

Analysis is both risky and scary. It can be like opening Pandora's box. We may find out things about ourselves we did not want to know. Areas for development stare at us like weaknesses in our character, and the list of things we are not so good at always seems longer than our list of achievements. The good news is that the more we undertake this type of analysis the less painful it becomes.

Like it or loathe it, risk is all around us and it pervades every aspect of our everyday lives. Every time a decision is made, there is a risk associated with the outcome. Risk is a major consideration in many industries which affect us directly, including:

● insurance – *eg* home and travel insurance costs

● financial markets – *eg* the value of pensions

● transport systems – *eg* aircraft and ferries

● security issues – *eg* policing issues.

There are risks associated with everything we do and it is important that we identify, analyse and manage the risks associated with our endeavours. The mundane drive to work is a potentially risky business. The car windows are iced-up and the ground is slippery underfoot. You identify a risk of icy road conditions. You check this by listening to a weather report which confirms the existence of black ice, and the fact that a number of accidents have already been reported. You therefore decide to:

● make sure you have good visibility

● allow the car to heat up to prevent windows misting

● use a main route to work as it is more likely to be wide, well lit and gritted.

The above set of actions demonstrates the process of identifying, analysing and finally managing the risk. Notice that you cannot reduce the risk of an accident to zero since you are at the mercy of other road users, but you can reduce it to 'as low as reasonably practical' (known as the ALARP principle).

Applying risk analysis

You will need to consider each of your skills development areas in this way. In some respects when performing a risk analysis on career prospects, you may feel you cannot win because there is a risk associated in doing nothing as well as the more obvious risk of proactively taking action. Consider the example of public speaking. Imagine that a member of staff had identified this as one of their negative skills and therefore in need of development. Now also imagine that one of their goals was 'To present the project plan to departmental management teams in September'.

Their first step should be to analyse the risk associated with this. This is done by constantly asking the question 'What if?'. It might look something like:

● What if I give a poor presentation?

● What if I mumble my words?

● What if I trip over the wires of the overhead projector?

● What if I mix up the overheads?

● What if I lose my train of thought?

● What if I am unable to answer questions?

– and so on. There is also the fact that in giving a poor presentation, the presenter does not appear competent at their job and may not even appear as future management material to the audience.

There are a number of corrective actions this person could put in place to manage the risk and thus reduce it. They could:

● take a short course in presentation skills

● ensure the room is set out correctly before they begin

● be organised in their approach and have all the right tools

● make sure they are properly prepared

● prepare in advance for a number of possible questions.

All this will not ensure that their presentation is faultless, but they will have the security of knowing that they have taken every step possible to minimise problems, and this confidence will add positively to their presentation.

Of course they could decide not to go through with it because they feel that the risk of it all going wrong is too great. However, as mentioned earlier, this decision also carries a risk. If they never attempt this presentation there is a possibility that they will:

● not achieve their goal

● not demonstrate their skills to others

● miss an opportunity to shine in front of key managers

● fail to add a key management skill to their portfolio

● feel a sense of failure.

Which risk would you take?

Performing a risk assessment

In performing a risk assessment on your proposed set of goals you need to decide if the goals you have set yourself are:

● feasible – does your social or family life allow you enough time to study for that college course?

● consistent – are your goals pulling in the same or opposite directions?

● complete – are the goals comprehensive enough to allow you to achieve that career move, or have you omitted an essential qualification?

● realistic – do you have the technical competence to complete that nuclear physics course or would you be better placed doing a foundation course?

● guarded by contingency – do you have a fallback position if certain goals are either not, or only partially, achieved?

Contingency planning

There may be good reasons why goals are either not fully met, or not in the way you planned; hence it is extremely useful to have a fallback position which allows you to salvage something positive. The provision of an appropriate contingency is an essential component of modern business practice, and the individual can use this technique to comprehensively enhance their capabilities and success factors, for with good contingency plans you need never fail!

For example, if you were relying on your organisation to pay for the training fees and for some reason this funding is no longer available – but you had already provisionally arranged a career loan with your bank – your training could still proceed.

There are very few 'jobs for life' in the current job market and we should expect to have to evolve and develop our skills throughout our working lives. Part of that evolution is the effective management of risks.

PRODUCING AN ACTION PLAN FOR YOUR DEVELOPMENT

You will now have two lists of skills: one in which you feel confident and are strong (positive skills), and one of skills which require developing (negative skills). Remember that even strong skills need exercising to ensure they remain at their best. The good news is that once you have developed a skill, just a little light toning from time to time will keep it sharp, whereas developing new skills can take some time. You will also have a list of your goals and the direction in which you want to move.

Just as you could not engage in ten hobbies simultaneously, you cannot attempt to take on too many new skills at once and expect to be fully competent in all. Look at your list: you must now begin to prioritise which skills, according to your goals, are the most important. The categories you should consider are set out in the first matrix in Figure 4.

You will see that your skills could fall into any of the four categories. They could be:

● very important and urgent

● very important but less urgent

● less important but urgent

● less important and not urgent.

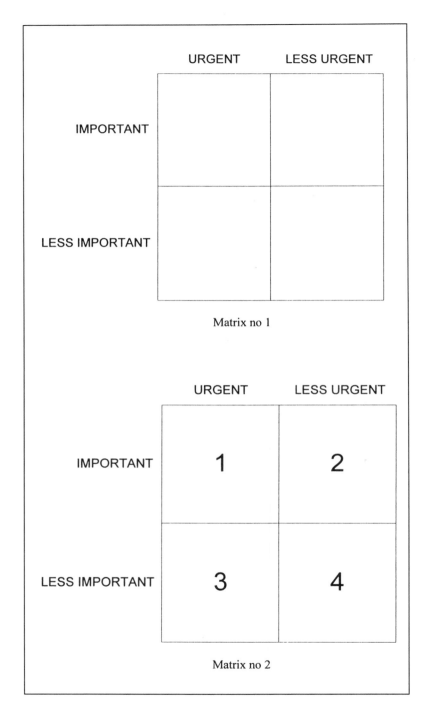

Fig. 4. Decision making matrices.

Copy the grid onto a large piece of paper and, with your goals in mind, write the names of your skills into the four boxes. Your priority for developing these skills should be as shown in the second matrix in Figure 4 with preference shown towards the importance of attaining the skills necessary to achieving those goals.

1. Firstly you will need to develop those skills which are very important in meeting your goals and the urgency is high (indicated with a figure one in the box). This could be acquiring presentation skills in time for a presentation to senior management next month.

2. The second priority (indicated by a figure two) should cover skills which are important but the urgency is less. This could be registering for a loan to cover the cost of a long term course, knowing that it will take quite some time to process the loan.

3. Your third priority is those skills which are of lesser importance to your immediate goals, but which still have urgency in your time frame (indicated by a figure three). An example of this would be signing up for a course which does not start until next year.

4. Those in the last category (indicated by a figure four) should be left for you to follow up at a later review, as neither their importance nor their urgency is key. It could be just re-flexing some of your skills which do not impact on your new goals.

When using this method of prioritising, be aware of the following things:

● time moves on – what is not urgent this month may be next month

● it is subjective – *you* make the decision which skill should be in each box

● situations change – you will need to review this regularly to ensure it is still valid.

You will now need a way of capturing this information in an action plan to store inside your career portfolio. Figure 5 shows an example of an action plan; however, there are many different templates and you may decide to design your own.

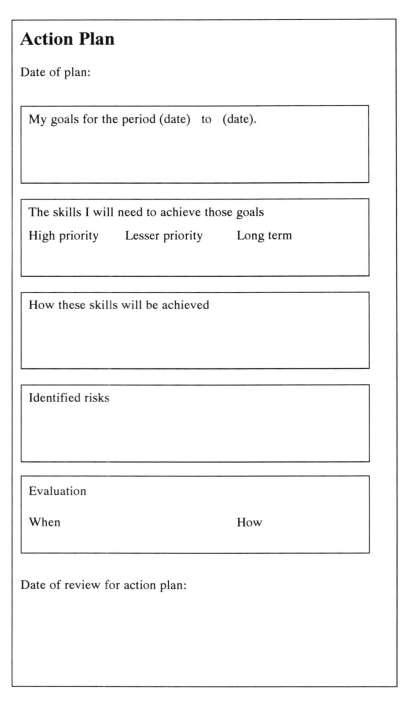

Action Plan

Date of plan:

My goals for the period (date)   to   (date).

The skills I will need to achieve those goals

High priority   Lesser priority   Long term

How these skills will be achieved

Identified risks

Evaluation

When   How

Date of review for action plan:

Fig. 5. A sample action plan.

PUTTING YOUR PLAN INTO ACTION

Your action plan is a meaningless piece of paper on its own. It is the word 'action' which should now be the focus. Many a good action plan has lain inside a drawer, never to see the light of day again. If this happens to your plan it would be a total waste of all the effort you have put in up to this point. You *must* take this plan forward to gain the positive results.

On the action plan shown in Figure 5, there is a box for you to suggest ways of progressing your plan (titled 'How these skills will be achieved'). The box should now be completed listing the different ways in which you plan to gain these skills. Some suggestions are given below.

External training

Colleges provide a range of courses which are increasingly being targeted at skills deficiencies rather than qualifications. One area where the two come together neatly is in National Vocational Qualifications (NVQs). These qualifications are work related and because you have to demonstrate competency in certain skills, they are proof that you can actually do the job. Contact your local college or training centre for a prospectus.

Internal training

If you work in a medium-to-large sized organisation, they are likely to provide an internal training prospectus or brochure. This training may be free to you as an employee, but will probably be limited to the skills which support the organisational goals rather than your personal ones. Contact your personnel or training department for details.

Distance learning

Distance learning has the advantage that it can be carried out anywhere, a positive bonus if you work away from home for long spells or spend your working day 'on the road'. Cassettes can be borrowed which cover a whole range of management skills, and also précis key management books. CD ROMS and computer based learning (CBL) can also be used effectively, but you will need regular access to a computer to complete the programme. If you have access to the Internet, you will find many distance learning courses advertised but there will be a charge for accessing them. Most libraries now contain a distance learning section and can obtain materials for you at little cost.

Books and periodicals

Books like this one are a great 'take anywhere' source of learning. There has been a growth in the number of books, periodicals and magazines aimed at gaining one specific skill or a defined group of skills, for example people management. They are a ready source of information which can be not only informative but also thought provoking. If you have not been inside a library for some time, take a look inside. You may be surprised at the broad range of literature available.

Project work

If you see one particular piece of work or project which would enable you to develop or further hone a certain skill, then approach your manager and ask to be involved. It is surprising how much you can learn even working on the periphery of a project. Project work is also an ideal opportunity to shine in a particular area. As project teams are pulled together to undertake a specific high level task, it will mean you are more exposed to senior staff than when performing your usual job.

Secondments

Secondments are when you work somewhere else for a period of time. They are an excellent way of reaching out and trying something new, or slipping into someone else's shoes for a while. They can be between departments or even between two different organisations. Secondments can also be for several days or a few years. A word of warning – if you decide to take this route for a long term secondment, ensure that you secure your return as out of sight can often be out of mind when reorganisations occur!

Workshadowing

Workshadowing is when you arrange with another member of staff to shadow their movements for a few days. You will need more than one day of workshadowing for two reasons:

1. One day is not really a reflective sample of the range of activities that a person undertakes in their job.

2. You will both have to relax into this as, at first, it may feel an unnatural situation on both sides.

   However, workshadowing can give you a valuable insight into how the person works, and the job they do. You may find that the job you coveted from afar is not quite what you thought when seen close to.

Voluntary work

This can cover any work which you undertake in your own time for no payment. Voluntary work encompasses all spheres and incorporates skill development, whilst providing a service to the community. In addition to charity work think about being a school governor, a magistrate, a councillor, or a youth leader.

'Sitting by Nellie'

The term 'sitting by Nellie' means sitting next to someone doing a job and copying them to learn that skill. It is the oldest form of training and can still be very effective. Children do it when they sidle up to parents and demand 'show me how to do that'. What better way to learn than by asking someone who has been performing a skill for many years? Take a look around you and think, who do you know who is really good at the skill you want to learn?

Back to the action

Complete the section on your action plan (titled 'How these skills will be achieved') by entering the methods you could, or will, use to achieve your high priority skills.

EVALUATION

Evaluation is the final tool in your toolkit. You will need to build some form of evaluation into planning your development to measure the success of your endeavours. You will need to assess whether:

● you have acquired the level of skill you set out to achieve

● you have completed it in the amount of time you set aside

● the skills were achieved at the planned cost

● your goals have been achieved.

Why evaluate?

Evaluation allows you to:

● monitor your progress

- reflect back on your experiences

- learn from your experiences

- forge ahead with confidence.

If you don't undertake any evaluation you will never know whether the investment of your time taken to acquire or maintain a skill was worth it. More importantly you will never be able to give yourself that well earned 'pat on the back' that you deserve.

The learning ring

Evaluation forms part of the 'ring of learning' as shown in Figure 6.

The ring demonstrates how, once you have planned to learn a skill, you will need to master it. Once achieved, you will have to integrate it into your work, which means practising it as part of your job. The final part of the ring is the evaluation section when you reflect on the process.

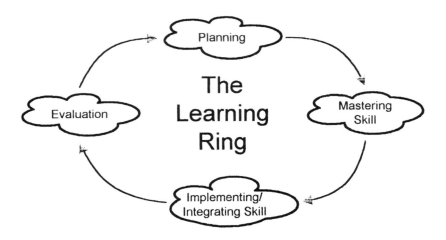

Fig. 6. The learning ring.

You will notice that after evaluation, and because it is a ring, you return to the planning section. This is because learning is cyclical – during the evaluation, when you reflect on your achievements and experiences, you will be planning your next set of goals. These new goals may emerge from circumstances taking you in a new direction, or they may be extending the same skills a little deeper.

Using evaluation

You may ask others to evaluate your new skills, or you may decide to undertake self evaluation.

Using others

Advantages	*Disadvantages*
They may be more proficient in the skill than yourself.	They may feel threatened by your new knowledge/skill.
They know the way you work.	You may outperform them.
They will know the 'old you' and will be able to assess the change.	They may give faint praise which can have a negative effect.

Self evaluation

Advantages	*Disadvantages*
You are your only judge.	Your measure of success is subjective.
Your measure of achievement is private.	You may be unsure of your evaluation skills.
You can target skills which go beyond those of your job without anyone knowing.	You will not benefit from the celebration of success that sharing an achievement can bring.

Documenting your evaluation

Your evaluation will need to be captured and logged, and will form another section in your portfolio (Chapter 5). Figure 7 shows a suggested format for performing an evaluation on the learning you have undertaken.

Evaluation of Learning

Course/Activity Title

Duration (including dates)

Which skills areas were covered by this activity?

How did this activity link to your personal goals?

What did you find most useful?

What did you find least useful?

How will you integrate these skills into your working practices?

How could you develop the skill further?

Fig. 7. Evaluation of learning.

CASE STUDIES

Richard takes the risk

Richard decides to try to produce a skills audit. He is unused to exposing so much of his life and worries that it might be a high risk venture. What if during the analysis he finds himself lacking in key skills?

Richard has only worked for one organisation, local government, but within that he has performed many roles. He therefore lists his roles when performing his skills audit. When he comes to analysing the audit he is surprised to find that some of his technical skills are not even used anymore. There is also a time lapse and he has to ask himself whether he could really claim to be competent in each skill. He decides to divide his skills into two headings, technical and non-technical. He also includes some of the training courses he has attended.

Carol takes control

Carol has held only one previous job, but she decides to reflect on the range of skills she gained through her life experiences. Whilst raising her three children Carol feels that she used a wide range of management skills including budgeting, motivation, team leading, planning, and effective time management. Although she would not expect anyone to promote her on the strength of these, they form an excellent base from which to build. Carol decides to set herself some firm goals for the following year and writes them in the front of her diary as a reminder. Also in her diary she makes a note to review them one year later. Carol starts to feel excited as she is actually taking control of her career.

Dean is unsure

Dean is unsure where to start. This is his first job and therefore he has few skills from work to start a list. He has not been on any training courses since joining his company. He pins the list on his bedroom wall and looks at it for two days. Out of the blue a friend from university visits and they spend some time reminiscing. He reminds Dean of some of the incidents they became embroiled in whilst Dean was chairman of the student's union. Suddenly Dean has something positive to add to his skills audit. His mother reminds him of the time out he took after university and the experiences he had – and he adds a little bit more. By building on ideas sparked by others, Dean now feels that he has enough to start planning the next phase.

POINTS TO CONSIDER

1.   Ask around. How many other people do you know who have action
      plans for their development?

2.   Think of three examples of companies who build their business on
      people's fear of taking risks?

3.   What is the difference between evaluation and reflection?

4
Making It Happen

Now you have your toolkit at your disposal, all you need to do is to get going. This is not always as easy as it sounds, so many good ideas never make it past the drawing board. As the great Chinese proverb says, 'Every long journey starts with a first step'. If you are not willing to take that first step then one thing is sure, you will never reach your destination.

MOTIVATING YOURSELF INTO ACTION

What makes you tick?

This is an easy question to ask, but it can be difficult to answer. However, it is worth spending some time trying to work out the answer since behind it lies the answer to your motivation.

Career conscious? Then it might be the opportunity of promotion which sparks you into action. Swayed by money? It may be the large pay cheque which promotion, or a new job, may bring. Often we may be made to feel embarrassed by placing such importance on one area of our lives. Especially if it is a seemingly superficial one. However, recognising and working with your own personal motivation factor is worthwhile. It helps us to harness our own motivational power and then use it to project us forward.

There is no need for anyone else to know this motivating factor. In fact in some circumstances you may feel that giving it away would be like showing all your trump cards, but although you keep it to yourself, you need to recognise its power.

Harnessing your motivation factor

Once recognised, anything linked to this motivating factor will stand a greater chance of success. For example, if you found you were working in your office every day to earn the money to travel, then by recognising this you could change your job so that you are paid to travel in work time. There are many opportunities in the travel/leisure industry, airline industry, and there are also project jobs working on European or international projects.

It is much easier instead to use this knowledge to work for you. If the need for more money is your greatest motivation, don't seek a new career in law because of the large salaries. You would have to go through many lesser paid years before you claw your way back past your current salary and into the higher earning category. Just recognising this has saved you from a major career mistake, which could prove difficult to explain on a CV.

If the need for more money is your prime motivation then you need to find a route to promotion (or a new job) in the shortest possible time, within your present profession.

EXERCISING THE BRAIN

Research has shown that the more you use the brain, the better it will function. It is a bit like flexing a muscle regularly; agility, speed and effective response are often increased. In the case of the brain, regular flexing and testing can increase memory, reasoned and creative thinking, and mental agility; in essence your mental capacity will increase greatly.

Exercising your brain power need not be by undertaking difficult equations or solving intricate mental puzzles. It can be achieved by simply introducing a slight change to some of your everyday practices.

Understanding left and right brain

The brain is divided into two halves which are connected by a complicated neural network. The left side of the brain is mainly involved with the formation of lists, numbers, logic and sequence. It controls your ability to speak, read, remember names, and enables rational thought.

The right side of the brain is more creative and emotional. It deals with spatial awareness, colour, rhythm and imagination. It is the side that enables play, daydreaming and creativity. Until fairly recently traditional school teaching was aimed firmly at the left hand side of the brain; however, research has now shown that if a mixture of right and left side qualities is used in parallel, this produces learning which is more effective.

Introducing colour into your work

Introducing colour into your note-taking can have a dramatic effect on increasing your memory. Next time you are going into a difficult meeting, take a set of coloured pens and start using them in your notes. If you feel this would not be acceptable, use highlighter pens to bring emphasis to certain points. A good tip is to use highlighter pens when revising for exams. It will be easier to remember certain points when they have been highlighted to catch the eye.

Bringing your notes to life

Your creative side of the brain (right side) loves pictures. It is for this reason that information which is transmitted through pictures is so often more appealing. Icons on computers have replaced rows of typed-in text, and suddenly more people are able to master file management. Next time you are taking notes, doodle some picture into the text so that you illustrate your thoughts. You don't need to be the great artist to draw extra pound signs (£) indicating an increase in the budget (or with minus signs in front for a decrease).

Useful symbols

Use symbols to illustrate text in future. In time you will develop your own form of shorthand. Try using some of the following:

? – don't understand this point, must ask later

* – this needs action by me after the meeting

! – a very important point, don't forget it

~ – this develops into this

∴ – therefore

< – lesser than

> – greater than.

You may decide to try incorporating some of these into your notes, but the greatest fun comes from producing your own. Think of some others you could use, for example a picture of a lightbulb to represent a good idea.

Mind Maps®

Have you ever been really stuck for ideas? Next time this happens to you, try Mind Maps, a creative thought technique designed by Tony Buzan. To study Mind Maps properly you will need to read one of Tony Buzan's books or contact Buzan Centres Ltd., (see Useful Addresses section), however, to get a flavour try the following exercise.

Use an illustration in the centre of a large white piece of paper (turned landscape) using at least three colours. As you concentrate on the central image thoughts will spring into your head. Write them on 'branches', radiating from the central issue like rays from the sun.

If one thought comes off another then show it as a branch from the original line. Don't worry if you write something which seems silly, or even the same thing twice, rationalisation of the data can be achieved later. Use symbols and pictures wherever you can to illustrate your thoughts.

This type of concentrated thinking exercise enables you to capture all your thoughts on paper as quickly and concisely as possible. It also enables you to allow your mind to wander (or radiate) around the issue, using both right and left sides of the brain. When the thoughts have stopped flowing you may decide to group your thoughts using dotted lines or highlighters, or edit some. To illustrate this technique an example is shown in Figure 8.

Sharpening your memory

Those who are memory masters assure us that everyone can have a good memory by using techniques for recall. There are several techniques which you might try; *eg* when remembering numbers, use a 'number rhyme' with mental pictures to help you. For example, 1 = bun, 2 = shoe, 3 = tree, 4 = door, *etc.* So if you are tying to remember the number 23 you might think of a shoe stuck in the top of a tree.

One technique for remembering names is this. When you are introduced to a person for the first time, repeat their name back in the first sentence, at the same time noticing them and perhaps noting their dress or any other distinguishing feature. If you can link the two (even in rhyme) then you will have a greater recall.

For example, 'May I introduce you to Mrs Helen Smith'. You would reply, 'Mrs Smith, how do you do?' At the same time you notice that she has black hair and is wearing a black suit. You make the mental connection with the key word 'blacksmith' by which you will remember her. If you wanted to follow this through further you could remember her first name by thinking of Hell being a very hot place, like the fires used by blacksmiths, and you conjure up a mental picture of the connection. As soon as it is acceptable you use her name again, for example, 'Mrs Smith (or Helen), may I take you over to meet our marketing manager, Mr Paine'. Now if I were Helen Smith I would be conjuring up either a picture of a pane of glass or feeling a pain in my leg to remember my next contact!

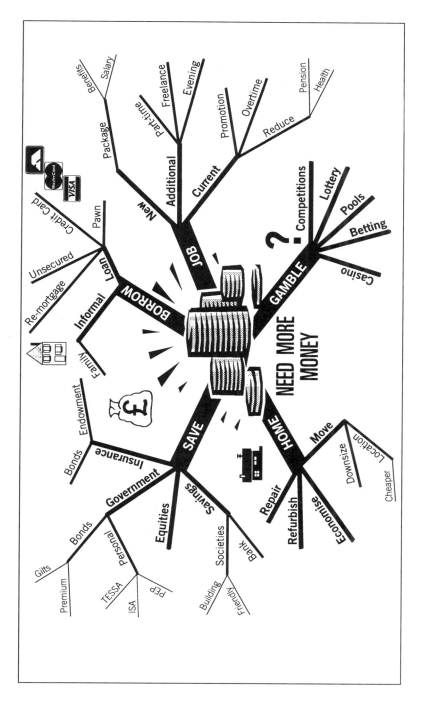

Fig. 8. Mind Map® diagram.

EXPLORING YOUR ENVIRONMENT

If you are considering a continuing career within your current organisation, ask the training (or personnel) department whether they have someone who would be willing to discuss career advancement opportunities with you. You will need to know early on in the process whether the future career you see mapped out for yourself is indeed within the scope of your organisation's future plans. If it isn't you will need to consider whether:

1. to change organisation

2. to tailor your career to what is available internally

3. your organisation is likely to move into that area of business within the foreseeable future.

As was stated earlier, predicting the future is not always possible but there may be pointers. Don't be shy, approach your manager or a more senior member of staff and ask them about the departmental or organisational business plan. It will give you a feel for the direction the company intends to take over the next five years and their current aims and values.

DEVELOPING YOUR SOFTER SKILLS

Soft skills are not only difficult to pinpoint, identify and describe, but they are also difficult to attain. Many training organisations will offer training courses in soft skills and although they will contain many handy tips and tricks, one cannot learn these skills overnight. If you attend a computer awareness course, it is most likely that you would return with a degree of competency (or measure of skill) on the computer. However, if you attend an assertiveness course you may return with a greater awareness, but still be unable to put it fully into action. We all develop personality traits which, even if we acknowledge their unsuitability to the situation, we find difficult to suppress or tailor.

Conventional training in these skills works on the basis of the person:

●   being aware of the 'problem'

●   understanding situations where this behaviour is likely to occur

- putting in 'blocking' or corrective mechanisms to enable them to make a different response

- reinforcing this through examples (possibly acting it out)

- feeding back to the group how it felt to be in better control of the situation.

There will need to be constant reinforcement in the workplace for that soft skill to feel natural. Soft skills are difficult to use and to practise, but they are the skills which employers are looking for today. It is not sufficient to be fully qualified, you need to handle people effectively and also practise a full range of other 'people skills', from showing empathy with a colleague to being assertive and challenging in meetings.

FEELING THE REWARDS

Are you starting to feel the rewards of your endeavours? Just feeling in control can be a positive experience. Perhaps you have not had that promotion just yet – after all it is early days. However, you should definitely be feeling the sense of power that *you* are making it happen – *you* are in control of this process.

Experiencing some movement in your career, or the feeling that something bold may happen, can be a bit scary. Many people are wary of change and it can be threatening to them to experience a change which is so close to themselves. In fact it may be themselves who are changing. Instead of thinking about 'changing', think about 'evolving' or 'growing' – this is not so threatening as most people readily accept the concept of all living things growing and flourishing. Without food, plants will die as will career growth without some form of regular input.

CASE STUDIES

Richard starts to consider his softer side

Richard is reflecting on the training he has undertaken since joining local government, but he had not considered his 'softer skills' as having any importance. He has been told on numerous occasions that he is good at talking to people, and 'has a way about him' when giving advice, but he had not capitalised on these as skills or thought how he would write them into his CV. He starts to think that maybe he has more to offer than his degree and a résumé of training courses.

Carol's notes take off

Carol decides to try using colour in her note taking. She is used to taking notes on white lined paper, but decides to use colour to emphasise certain facts. She buys a pack of coloured pens and a couple of highlighters, and keeps them in a bag to take to meetings. At first it seems strange to use colour, and she certainly attracts attention amongst her colleagues, but she soon finds out that when reviewing her notes or typing them up later, her recall of the meeting is vastly improved.

Dean explores his motivation

Dean realises he might have to make a significant change to his attitude and the style in which he lives, if he is to develop himself for promotion. He decides to examine his motivation to find out whether it is strong enough to keep his focused. He thinks long and hard about what he hopes to get out of the extra effort needed. If he puts the time in, what is in it for him? Is it worth it? He decides his main motivation factor is to gain a promotion for himself, which he accepts is centred on his personal need for esteem and recognition. A side issue is that it will also net him additional income and mean that he can set up home with his girlfriend.

POINTS TO CONSIDER

1. Colour code your filing system at work. Locating files will be so much easier if they are in coloured groups.

2. Each time you meet someone new try to find out one interesting thing about them. They will be flattered with the attention, and you are more likely to remember them (including their names).

3. Ask colleagues to tell you what they think you are particularly good at. You may be surprised by their observations.

5
Taking the First Steps

The first steps of any new project can be scary. They are fraught with 'what ifs'. If that new project is **you**, then they can be doubly so. Remember, you cannot go wrong on this one. Each move you make from now on will take you one step nearer your goals. You need to:

- consider the opportunities

- refine your action plan

- collate a portfolio

- start making first contacts.

CONSIDERING THE OPPORTUNITIES

All around you there are opportunities for your development. Use the method of Mind Maps (in Chapter 4) to explore a number of opportunities which might take you nearer to each goal. Use a separate Mind Map for each goal, or skill, and place it in the centre of the page – then let your imagination radiate out from that focus like the one shown in Figure 9.

Making your selection

After performing this exercise you will have a number of 'maps'. These Mind Maps may vary from just a few options to showing many different ways of reaching your goals. It is from these that you will make your choice.

In the first instance cast your eyes over the Mind Map and cross out any which are not feasible, or were 'fantasy' suggestions. For example, placing all your faith in winning the lottery is not a realistic solution when facing current debt.

REFINING YOUR ACTION PLAN

Take another look at your action plan. Be clear where you are going to start, you now need a tight focus to make clear, sure decisions.

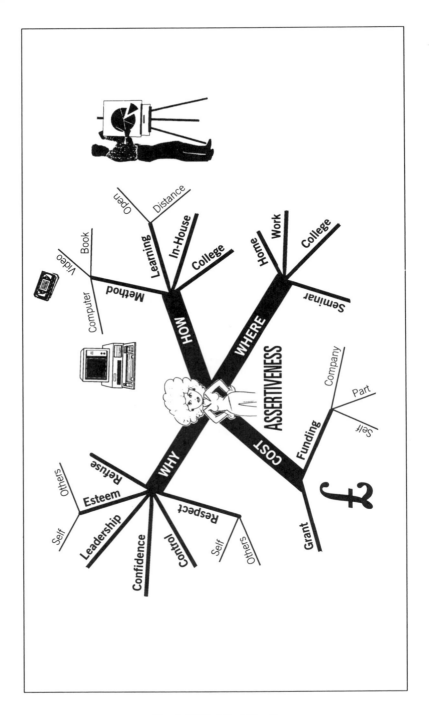

Fig. 9. Skills Mind Map®.

In performing the prioritising exercise (in Chapter 3) you will have decided which skills are both urgent and important, and therefore should receive immediate attention. Look at these again, they will be your focus in the short term.

How do they fit with your Mind Map exercise? Have you discovered realistic methods for attaining these skills?

You are refining your action plan to form a decision on your course of development. Your choice of development must be CORRECT:

Cost efficient – Who is paying for this? Is it affordable?

Opportune – It is available when you want it?

Realistic – Can it be realistically achieved?

Relevant – It is relevant to your future career?

Effective – Will it give you the skills you need?

Comfortable – Are you at ease with this choice?

Timely – Is there a 'right' time for doing it?

Use the CORRECT checklist to help through each skill and the best way of attaining it. Add any notes you make to your other diagrams, maps and action plans. They will make valuable reference later, and you will be able to track the reason for your decisions, when reflecting.

Using the CORRECT method above will help you to decide which method of development will be the most appropriate for you in each instance.

STEPPING OUT

You have your action plan charting your personal career development. You also now have your ideal method of attaining these skills. Now you need to pull together the actual information on how you are going to put your method of development into operation. If you have selected using a book as your method for learning negotiating skills then you need to obtain it somehow. You could buy it or borrow it from a library, but until you enquire about the price or how long it will take the library to obtain it, you cannot decide which course to take.

Likewise if you decided on a college course on training skills, you will need to know the start date, where it is available and the contents of the syllabus before you can sign up.

Stepping out is about gathering the background information together so that you are literally ready to go. It may mean filling out forms, getting a signature or arranging a career loan. Stepping out is about commitment. It's about saying, 'I've committed myself to this course of action'. It's about no going back!

> **Stepping out is your development in action.**

RECORDING YOUR PROGRESS

All your notes and diagrams will amount to a significant input of work. To preserve this investment, your action plan, charts and notes should be collated in one place, so that:

● they are easy to refer back to

● they are protected and the paper not screwed up

● they are all together in one place for easy referral

● they can be taken, collectively, into an appraisal or interview session.

Your portfolio

You are now in the position to build your own portfolio. This is simply a place where you will store the information regarding your career development. It could be a ring binder or a box file, but it is important that it is in the format you will find easiest to use, and that it reflects you. It can be any colour, but a word of warning about cartoon decoration. Unless you are in advertising or a profession connected with the media, cartoons designs adorning a portfolio can appear frivolous and unprofessional.

Making it accessible

Use dividers or coloured tabs to section up the information. Clearly label each one 'CV', 'Action Plan', etc. This will make it easier to reference, for example during an interview, when you are bound to be nervous; and it will help you to file information away quickly.

Label the front or side with your name and the contents, for example:

John Matthews
Personal Portfolio

or

Jean Jarvis
Career Information

Use plastic pockets if there are particular pieces of work that you handle regularly. It will save them from finger marks.

Filing other information

In future when you feel inspired by an article in a business magazine or publication, cut it out and file it in your portfolio. Although you do not want to collect too many of these, it can be impressive to others that you gain inspiration from reading. It also demonstrates that you keep abreast of your profession by reading periodicals.

Include a copy of your latest CV and ensure that it is updated regularly to reflect your current situation. Although many jobs require the applicant to complete a prescribed form, interviewers are often keen to also see a CV as it allows you free rein to display your talents.

Storing your portfolio

Your portfolio is best stored where it is most accessible. Whether this is in the office or at home, it is important that it is somewhere prominent rather than hidden in a drawer. If you see it regularly, it will remind you to visit it now and again. If it is hidden away, you have provided yourself with the perfect excuse for forgetting about it.

MAKING FIRST CONTACTS

To step out effectively you will need to contact other people. Whether you are speaking to a tutor or approaching someone at work you will need that initial first contact.

Quite often people will refer you to others not realising how difficult it is to make that initial contact with an unknown person. It is not surprising that our fear of rejection makes us 'bottle out' and very often we don't bother to approach the person at all. If that happens who is the loser? **We are!** That person may have held the answer to all our problems – but now we will never know.

There are many books available on conquering our fear of approaching others, but the easiest method is:

● introduce yourself giving your name, job title and organisation

● state who has referred you to them and why

● let them know **clearly** what you are asking of them

● then, let the person answer.

The dialogue should flow, for example:

'Hello, my name is Sally Hopkins and I am a project officer at Midshires Bank. My colleague Bill Williams has given me your number because I am looking into the effects of change and he knew you had undertaken a large change in your organisation. I wondered whether you would be able to spend some time discussing it with me?'

The person on the other end of the phone has all the information up front, and can make a decision whether or not to allow the conversation to continue.

If the person tells you that they cannot help you, then never ring off before asking whether they know of anyone else who would have the information. Quite often projects are passed from one person to another, people change jobs, and it is not always easy to locate the right person first time.

If finally the person does not want to help you, then simply thank them for their time before ringing off.

Remember – at the end of the call thank the person for their time. It always pays to be polite as you may meet them at a later date. Time is a most precious commodity which cannot be recouped, so thank them for allowing you some of their valuable time.

CASE STUDIES

Richard steams ahead
Richard is good at approaching and talking to people and decides that, working in local government, there are likely to be plenty of opportunities for other people to help him in his development. He contacts his training department to find out whether they are able to help him find people in other departments with similar feelings about development.

Carol gets organised

Carol is very organised. She sees the value in keeping all her development notes in one place and decides to design a portfolio before she has to push all her papers in a folder. She considers the image she wants to create and chooses a suitable cover. She draws up a contents list and then makes neatly labelled dividers for each section. She decides to keep it on her desk where she has easy access to it, and she does not mind others seeing it too. In fact it has prompted several conversations with senior people who have seen it and been intrigued.

Dean catches on

Dean does not want to go back to college and so is delighted to find out there are so many other ways of developing yourself. He is drawing diagrams and examining his action plan, and is enjoying the fun element. He has involved his girlfriend in many of the exercises, and she is now getting interested in her own personal development. They both seem to have been bitten by the bug.

POINTS TO CONSIDER

1. Re-visit your action plan and complete the section on how you plan to attain these skills.

2. Produce your own portfolio which reflects your style.

3. Before contacting someone for the first time, make a Mind Map focused on what you are going to ask them.

6
Finding a Mentor or Coach

Often other people seem to have the skills we desire. They may possess particular skills or use limited skills to best effect. Perhaps they hold the position we want or have followed a similar career path with great success. It is important to identify these people as they can help considerably in taking the fast track route towards career success.

WORKING WITH SOMEONE ELSE

When deciding to work with someone else, both people should ultimately benefit. Twice the benefits for one relationship – what a great deal!

Indeed it is important that there is something in the relationship for both parties, if it to continue and thrive. Relationships where one party does all the taking are likely to cause resentment and may end on bad terms. The relationship and the manner in which it is conducted through to the end are as important as the learning and should be given equal consideration.

Involving others in your development entails forming complex relationships which, although not always easy, have hidden benefits which cannot be gained by textbooks alone. People can introduce you to the movers and shakers in an organisation. They can open doors for you which may otherwise be closed. They can introduce you to a whole new network of people, each of whom have their own unique mix of skills, and hold valuable information.

USING A MENTOR

Mentoring is a valuable method for gaining personal support for self development and self managed learning. The role of the mentor is to help the individual to gain deeper insights into how to handle the complexities and opportunities which present themselves in the workplace.

Mentors are often more senior than the individual seeking personal support, but this need not always be so. Also mentors need not be from the same organisation. In fact on occasions it is more appropriate for the mentor to be someone from 'outside'. What is essential is that the individual seeking support should respect the mentor and their opinions, so that they can feel confident that the mentor will provide them with the level of support they need.

Identifying a mentor

If your organisation has a mentoring system you may be able to select from a 'bank' of self nominated people who are willing to be mentors. If this is not the case then it is a matter of identifying a mentor who will be able to help. Through asking around (colleagues and the personnel department), some names may arise, or you may immediately know who you would approach.

Look for someone who:

● is known for developing people

● has a wide range of skills to share

● has a wide network of contacts

● is interested in helping people progress

● identifies with your situation by being in either the same organisation or the same field

● is patient and has good interpersonal skills

● is willing to devote time to the relationship

● has your respect.

Think through the mentor's situation before approaching them. It may be that they are a senior manager who is used to taking major decisions. They may find it difficult to stand back and encourage you through your own decision making. Similarly, they may already have huge constraints on their time, and be working too many hours to give quality time to the relationship.

Understanding how mentors work

Mentors do not give flat advice and guidance on problems the individual may be facing at work. They work on the individual, not on the work problem.

A mentor can help an individual to:

● reflect on what they have done

● adapt their behaviour and approach

● explore new ways of dealing with situations.

They also:

● provide encouragement and support

● give constructive feedback.

It may also be possible for the mentor to provide a greater in-depth knowledge of the organisation and how it works.

APPROACHING SOMEONE TO WORK WITH YOU

It is not always easy to approach someone to work with you. Not everyone understands mentoring and it can be easy for the relationship to turn into a chatty friendship from which neither party benefits other than from information passed through idle gossip. A relationship formed in this way will soon come to a close, with possible resentment and disappointment on both sides. For this reason it is helpful if the person who is to be the mentor has either an understanding of the mentoring relationship or previous, positive experience.

Finding such a person will not be easy, and then it is likely that if they actively support mentoring, they will already be in a mentoring relationship with someone else. It is better to anticipate that the mentor you choose to approach is unlikely to have experience and therefore you will need to educate them in the first instance.

Making your approach
The first contact can be made:

● by phone

● by appointment

● by letter.

If the mentor is a more senior person it may not be easy to contact them by phone. They may have secretaries or assistants who will use all manner of techniques to ensure you do not speak to the person direct. If this is the case then the second attempt should be to try and make an appointment. Approaching the person face-to-face is very effective and allows you to explain the relationship (and commitment) fully, and them to ask all the questions they wish. If this is also not possible then approach them through a letter. Do not try and explain too much in the letter, just arouse their interest and again request an appointment to meet with them. An example is shown in Figure 10.

Do not be surprised if the mentor wants to take time to consider all the facts and does not give you an immediate answer. It is a major commitment on both sides and the start of a 'forced' relationship which may have not come about any other way.

A lengthy period of consideration should be viewed as a positive indication of how seriously they are willing to take this, and therefore of the depth of their commitment to making the relationship work.

USING A COACH

Coaching skills have only recently been recognised as skills which transfer from the sports field into management. Coaching has always been valued in sport as a way of helping people reach their potential. Coaching skills are now being recognised as transferable into the office environment. Sports coaches, although knowledgeable about their sport, are not necessarily former superstars. Their most important skill is knowing how to get the best out of another human being. How to encourage them to go the extra mile or give it that final last try.

Coaches may hand out advice or information, but their expertise lies in understanding people and introducing some processes which help them to work through their problems, and encourage progress. They believe in the power of positive thought as being a significant factor in a person's success.

Finding a coach

Few organisations integrate coaching into their management requirements at present although indications are that they are moving in that direction. Managers of the future will need to coach their staff to get the best from them. Coaching skills will be highly prized and become integrated into management training. However, in the meantime it may not be possible to locate a coach within the organisation.

There are consultancies who provide a coaching service, but these

Bowater Scott
The Red House
Bringsden
BR99 8PP

Paul Madey
Operations Manager
Housing Section

30 September 199X

Dear Paul

You may be aware that I am putting a considerable effort into my
personal development. As part of a self analysis programme I
have identified the need for a mentor to help me gain a greater
understanding of my actions and also provide an in-depth
knowledge of the organisation.

I would like to meet with you to discuss the possibility of you
undertaking that role. This would also include talking through
how the arrangement would work in practice, the level of
commitment, and answer any questions you might have. I
understand that you have severe time constraints and therefore I
will ring you in a few days' time for your initial reaction to this
proposal, and perhaps set a date to meet.

Regards

Mike Morgan

Fig. 10. Sample mentoring letter.

can be expensive. Depending on your current earning power they may be completely out of the question in terms of affordability and you need to calculate the quality of the coaching skills against your progression in the same way you would assess any return on an investment.

CHARTING THE RELATIONSHIP

Mentoring and coaching are development tools which can be beneficial to both parties. For this reason it is best practice to test out one another's expectations of the relationship and agree a set of ground rules such as confidentiality, frequency of meetings and so on.

Meetings can be for any length of time and frequency depending on the need and flexibility of both parties. It may be that longer infrequent meetings are more suitable than shorter regular meetings, or vice versa.

During the first phase of the relationship, the person receiving the mentioning/coaching may have unrealistic expectations of the relationship. They often hold the mentor/coach in high esteem, seeing them as highly competent and are generally enthusiastic about the outcomes of the relationship. There are usually positive expectations on both sides.

Reaping rewards

It is the middle period of the relationship that is usually the most rewarding. The friendship and sense of trust have been strengthened and a high degree of intimacy will have developed. Results are being recognised and acknowledged on both sides. It is also during this period that the mentor/coach gains great satisfaction from the development of the person on the receiving end, similar in feeling to parental pride. It is a particularly rich stage for both parties.

Managing the end of the relationship

The ending of the relationship can come in several ways:

● the relationship has run its course

● changes within the organisation affect the relationship

● the person receiving the support achieves their objective

● there is interference in the relationship from a third party

● the relationship is disjointed, *eg* long term sickness on either side

- one party is not happy with the way the relationship is developing

- one party moves work/area.

However the relationship ends, it is far more constructive if that ending is managed rather than just allowed to happen. Towards the end of the relationship, the mentor/coach becomes less essential to the person who is receiving guidance. Depending on the way in which the end occurs, the person receiving the mentoring/coaching can feel either that they have outgrown the relationship or deep anxiety that the mentor/coach is no longer there. Similarly it can be difficult for the mentor to accept that their protégé needs to stand alone or move on.

The most positive way to end a learning relationship is to call a final meeting whereby both parties meet with an agenda to discuss and express frank feelings about the end of the relationship. The agenda should also cover the achievements on both sides and the learning that has taken place. Mentoring relationships require the same degree of consideration that would be afforded any personal relationship and each party owes it to the other to ensure that this is of prime concern.

Meeting rejection

Be prepared for possible rejection as not everyone will want to enter into a learning relationship with you. There are a variety of reasons for this. At one end of the scale they may fear your success and, at the other, they may simply not have the time to spare. There is also the possibility that they are involved in a similar learning relationship which has first call on their time and thought processes.

If your approach is rejected do not consider it a personal slight. Identify clearly what you hoped to gain from the relationship, and seek another who will be able to satisfy those criteria.

Returning the favour

You may be wondering, if someone is giving you a proportion of their time and information for free, what can you offer in return? Many people just like helping others to reach their potential, but there are also other factors which they may also like to explore. Becoming a mentor or coach can also add to their development and are considered valuable skills in today's environment. They can use the meetings to sharpen joint problem solving skills and communication. In larger organisations it helps the mentor or coach, who is usually a senior person, to keep in touch with the 'grass roots' within the organisation. It can also help them in their role as a manager by enabling them to maintain an understanding of the issues affecting others. In addition one should not underestimate the reflected pride felt in enabling another person to excel and reach their goals.

CASE STUDIES

Richard gets a surprise

Richard feels that mentoring or coaching is inappropriate for him. He has a very broad knowledge of his organisation and has worked at a senior level in several departments. He was just reflecting on the people he has worked with when he is interrupted by a phone call from Susan in the personnel department. She has been thinking of starting a mentoring programme within the organisation and wondered whether, with his experience, he would be willing to train to be a mentor. Richard was most surprised. He had not thought of mentoring someone else, but was able to impress Susan with his knowledge of mentoring, and offered to help her design the programme.

Carol decides to get help

Carol feels that she needs some inside information. Since joining the Northern Bank she has been impressed by a female manager who had started in the organisation in a similar clerical support role to hers. She decides to approach the manager direct to see whether she would be interested in entering a mentoring arrangement. In preparation, Carol draws a Mind Map of all the points she wants to raise, then she makes the phone call. The manager is both surprised and flattered by Carol's request and makes a date to meet her for lunch to discuss it further.

Dean goes outside

Dean cannot think of anyone with whom he would feel comfortable in a mentoring relationship. He feels that his whole life needs an overhaul and decides instead to go to an outside coach. He approaches several companies and asks for fees and references. Dean is prepared for the coach to make suggestions about his finances and his lifestyle, in addition to giving him career advice. He believes he is making a calculated investment in his future, and hopes his investment will pay off in the future.

POINTS TO CONSIDER

1. Think of a scenario when you would definitely use a coach in preference to a mentor.

2. Describe how you would feel if a friend who you wanted to be your mentor refused your offer.

3. Think of two possible mentors. How would you approach each of them? Would it be different in each case or the same?

7
Moving up a Gear

Now your development is taking off you are ready to take on board some more ideas for further skills development. Some you may have thought of, others may be new to you. This chapter gives you more dynamic ways of developing soft skills and therefore moving nearer to your goals.

CONSIDERING OTHER DEVELOPMENT OPPORTUNITIES

Consider looking outside the organisation for different development opportunities. Many skills are transferable across different sectors as long as you are able to pinpoint them and substantiate the link.

Seeking public appointments

Public appointments offer a considerable range of development opportunities. Every year many people take on public appointments in addition to their daily jobs. One of the reasons may be that it allows them responsibilities which are not afforded them in their day-to-day job. That may be handling a large budget, responsibility for recruiting staff, or taking major decisions. Viewed in this way, public appointments make very good development opportunities. One point to remember is that they are a severe time commitment which cannot be terminated at will, so think carefully before committing yourself to a role which is too demanding for your lifestyle. Below is a brief selection of public appointments and an indication of the skills they offer:

- **School governor** – Skills: budget handling, recruitment, performance at meetings, decision making.

- **Magistrate** – Skills: decision making, analysis, legal, interpersonal.

- **Councillor** – Skills: communication, debating, decision making, political.

Working with trusts and charities

Trusts and charities are always on the look out for trustees, board members, and volunteers who will take an active role in running the business. Voluntary organisations are different from public and private organisations. As the work is unpaid, skills can be quickly obtained 'on the hoof' if you are willing to give the time. Naturally if you have a profession or particular line of work, they may prefer you to be in that role, but there is every opportunity to branch out into a different role, a situation quite unlikely to happen in the paid work situation.

One word of warning. Before joining *any* voluntary organisation ensure that you understand the level and parameters of your responsibility, and that any financial liability is covered by insurance.

Becoming involved in institutes

Most professions are headed by an institute. Many people join the institute covering their profession because it gives them a number of benefits such as letters after their name, free legal advice, access to specialist libraries, and regular journals. Most professional institutes run events which range from evening talks and meetings through to full training days. If your development need is in a specific area or covers a particular topic, contact the institute you think may be able to help. For example if you want to know more about marketing then contact the Institute of Marketing. It does not matter if you are not a member, they will put you in touch with the appropriate region which will very likely invite you along to its next event to help swell the numbers.

The regional subsections of institutes are run by committees. These committees are also often run by the faithful few, and always welcome new members. This does not mean that you have to take the chair immediately, but if you are looking at brushing up your budgeting, event organising, or minute taking skills, you would be sure to find a warm welcome. Similarly if you would like to work on your presentation skills, then institutes are always on the look-out for original speakers to attend their events.

Specialist interest groups (SIGs)

Whatever club, institute or group you may belong to it is likely that they will have a special interest group. These groups are put together to either debate an issue (and then disband) or pursue an off-shoot interest of the main group. For example, a regular meeting of personnel professionals may start a special interest group around 'sexual harassment at work' as, perhaps, an issue for debate or a personal issue for those involved. If becoming an expert in this area would benefit your development then involvement within this group would be beneficial.

If you don't know of any SIGs which would benefit your development, but like the idea, then start your own. Advertise your topic around the organisation or invite particular people to come to a lunchtime session. You may start a new trend, and the experience in organising these will be, in itself, developmental.

TAKING THINGS OUTSIDE

Everything discussed so far has been focused on learning more about your organisation and using internal methods of development. However, many other organisations are realising the benefits of opening doors and sharing ideas and opportunities. Secondments, joint seminars/workshops, shared training are all examples of organisations working together. Taking advantage of these opportunities benefit:

1. **You** – you will see how other organisations think and act.

2. **Your organisation** – you will return with fresh ideas and be able to relate these to the workplace.

3. **Their organisation** – they will learn from you, your experience, and different perspective.

Finding the right organisation

The right organisation will be one that appreciates the values of learning and is willing to share its experiences – in essence a 'learning organisation'. It will also be an organisation which either follows good practice in the area you want to observe or specialises in that topic. If this arrangement is to become part of your CV then it must convey the right image and portray successful outcomes.

If you have researched your topic or area thoroughly or it is akin to your current profession you probably know of a number of excellent companies with whom you would like to work. However, if you are branching out into a new area, then you may not know whom to approach.

To find out which organisations are leading the field, use professional colleagues and institutes. For example the Institute of Management (see Useful Addresses at the back of this book) holds a wealth of information regarding the largest and most influential companies. If you want details of companies within your country, your library holds records, together with their addresses and phone numbers. The Department of Trade and Industry (see Useful Addresses) also offers advice and local contact points within your area.

Approaching other organisations

Approaching another organisation needs thought and planning prior to the initial phone call. If you have a contact within the organisation then it can be quite simple to locate the right person, but from a cold phone call it can be difficult to get your message across. This stage must not be rushed if it is to succeed.

First of all phone the organisation on their main switchboard number, and ask for a copy of their company brochure or pack of information to be sent to you. If you are clear about the department you want to work with, you could also ask for the name of the head of that department. Always ask the operator to confirm the spelling of the name and the address. Incorrect spelling of names offends and shows lack of preparation, and their site address may be different from that of head office.

If you are not sure about the department or person you will need, ask for the name and address of the Head of Personnel, Human Resources Manager, or Learning Adviser, and confirm their correct job title. Write to this person in the first instance. They will be able to either deal with your enquiry or send it to the most appropriate manager. A suggested letter is shown in Figure 11.

If you hear nothing from the organisation, it would then be appropriate to phone and ask whether the person had received the original letter and considered its contents. You could also suggest at this point that you meet with someone to discuss matters further.

Organising your learning

To enter any serious discussion with another organisation you will need the following:

● the full backing of your manager and/or present organisation (a prerequisite for any external collaborations)

● a clear set of objectives demonstrating what you want to achieve

● the skills you hope to gain from the experience

● benefits the host organisation will gain from entering into this arrangement (eg a local government perspective on a private industry issue)

BCD Computing
BCD House
Lower Hampton
LH9 00P

Mr P Richards
Head of Personnel
RJS Ltd
The Strand
Upper Hampton
LH10 00J

30 September 199X

Dear Mr Richards

I have a strong interest in personal development and have
identified a gap in my skills profile around matrix management.
I understand that RJS Ltd has considerable experience in this
area, built up over a number of years. I would like to meet with
you to discuss any opportunities which may result in joint
working, specifically around matrix management. I will ring you
in a few days to discuss this further and make an appointment.

Yours sincerely

R Hicks

Fig. 11. Sample letter of approach.

● a proposal as to how this will happen (secondment, workshadowing, interviews, *etc*).

No organisation will spend time in discussions unless you have a clear focus, know what you are asking for, and have permission to make it happen. This is a project and requires planning in the same way as any other project. The difference is that this project is a little closer to home in that it concerns your development.

Selling the benefits
Selling the benefits to the host organisation is often the crucial point of persuasion. There has to be something in it for them to agree to any arrangement which incurs the time and patience of their staff. It may be the bonus of an 'end product' which they may use, for example an evaluation or comparative study between your organisations, which may remain internal or could be published. Another example would be offering a perspective from a different industry on a live issue or problem. Another payback could be a reciprocal arrangement whereby they send someone to work in your organisation. In future this could develop into a partnership arrangement which would be beneficial to both organisations.

BUILDING RELATIONSHIPS

When you contact another organisation you are automatically building complex relationships which can be just as volatile as human relationships. These should not be entered into lightly and must be controlled and examined periodically. There are the relationships between the people in the two (or more) organisations, and there are also the relationships between the organisations themselves. Some organisations do not want to be seen openly talking to other organisations, particularly competitors. Others want to build strong relationships, and may even ask for more than your organisation is prepared to give.

It is also important that all communication between organisations is conducted in a civil and proper manner, and the people concerned respond professionally. Relationships cannot flourish and grow where there is conflict.

Asking the right questions

Periodically all relationships need re-evaluating. This is not to say that if the relationship no longer satisfies its original intention, then it should be ended. Rather it is to ensure that the relationship continues to be of value, even though other factors may change.

Asking the following questions will help you to evaluate the relationship:

1. How long has the current relationship been maintained?

2. Are there regular review points for all parties?

3. What was the feeling at the last review (positive? unsure?)?

4. Is the original reason for the relationship still required?

5. Can the relationship be developed or extended in any way?

6. How would all parties see the relationship developing over the next three/five years?

Occasionally relationships do run their course and reach a natural conclusion, and if that is the wish of both parties then an evaluation of the learning should take place (see Evaluation, Chapter 3, and Reflecting on the experience, Chapter 10). This will enable all parties to celebrate the achievements gained by the relationship and end it positively.

NETWORKING

Networking is one of the buzzwords of today. It is based on the principle that people need people. Networks can be small or large, and formal or informal. You may be invited to join an established network or you could create your own.

The benefits of being part of a network include:

● the potential for gaining new knowledge

● the sharing and developing of knowledge

● information gained through communication and interaction with people

● social interaction and personal visibility.

Any situation where people are interacting with other people to convey information is a network.

Networking power

Networks can be very powerful. Access to a network which includes very senior managers can provide the kind of exposure not normally afforded to those lower in the hierarchy. Therefore any opportunity to be present at such an event should be accepted. Networks are also powerful in that an enormous amount of information can be conveyed very quickly.

Networking for yourself

Creating your own network is essential, it will allow you to build a bank of information specifically tailored for your needs. Your personal network is built up of people who can provide you with the information needed to expand your knowledge base, both technical and social. They will introduce you to others who will help you, and will have their own network to tap into.

Points for networking

● When you meet someone for the first time or are introduced, smile, look them in the eye and shake their hand whilst saying your name clearly.

● Always carry business cards so that you can pass them around at events or hand one over after an introduction.

● Try to meet in an informal setting. Meeting in an office can quickly turn formal, especially if it is your first meeting.

● When you are introduced to someone new, try to find out as much information as you can about them: where do they work, who do they know? You may find that you have a colleague in common.

● Ask for a business card before leaving. If they don't have one ask for their phone number and make a note of it.

● Keep it light. Don't hassle anyone to get back in contact with you. Networking is voluntary and has to have the agreement of both parties to continue and flourish.

● Maintain a network section in your diary or portfolio to log names and phone numbers.

KEEPING THE MOTIVATION GOING

Self development is hard work. Networking, recording your experiences, using mentors, and learning from others takes a lot of time – and on top of that you have a job! It is no wonder that your development portfolio can find its way to the back of the shelf, and stay there.

If you feel your motivation slipping then get out your portfolio right now. Dust it off and read through your CV and your action plans. Focus on what you have achieved rather than the completion dates you may have missed. Look at how far you have come. If you remain unsure, ask your manager, or a colleague you trust, whether they have detected an improvement in your performance since embarking on the journey of self development. Finally you should speak to your mentor, or a trusted person from your network. It is likely they have felt the same at some point in their life and may be able to help.

Using rewards

Just as people are encouraged to lose weight by the thought of a new outfit, reward yourself for every achievement. Celebrating achievements is a wonderful way of reminding yourself of the hard work involved and recognising the effort you have put in. Don't wait for a close colleague or partner to suggest celebrating your every achievement. You cannot expect them to be as excited as you. So next time you win a contract through your network, or you finish a workshadowing exercise, open a bottle of wine, go out for a meal, or buy yourself a book – whatever is appropriate. Celebrate that success. It will increase your motivation and keep you focused.

CASE STUDIES

Richard goes public

Richard has more time on his hands now that his children have left home. He decides that some of that time could be put to better use by doing some voluntary work, but he does not want it to infringe on his daily job. He contacts a local charity, which gives him a warm welcome and invites him for a chat. As their meetings are during the evening they will not encroach on Richard's daytime job, and they need people to undertake the kind of roles totally new to Richard. After talking it through with his wife, he decides on a trial period of three months.

Carol gets networking

Carol starts to look at her organisation in a new way. She counts up the number of women in all levels of the organisation and the results surprise her. The number of women in senior management is severely lacking. Carol decides to approach the personnel department about setting up a women's network to support women in their career with Northern Bank, and to help them break through the 'glass ceiling'. Naturally Carol hopes that the network will help her development too, as she will gain useful exposure to many senior staff.

Dean recognises his networks

Dean is not interested in voluntary work or public duties, he is either busy working or socialising. However, as part of his work he is supposed to attend a monthly meeting of all computer professionals. Dean has not gone for the last three months because he found it had become boring with the same 'old' faces. Dean suddenly realises that rather than stopping going to these meetings he should have played a more active part, using the knowledge gained from his Student Union role to enhance and promote the meetings. He decides to phone the organiser with some of his ideas, such as changing them into networking meetings, having specialist speakers and setting up special interest groups.

POINTS TO CONSIDER

1. How many special interest groups do you know in existence? If not many, contact the institute covering your profession and find out.

2. Find out which other organisations have professional links with your own organisation?

3. Are you part of a network? If not, why not?

8
Making Sure You are Using Your Full Potential

Every so often it makes sense to return to your portfolio and revise the steps you have taken. Are you sure you are using your full potential? Have you tried a spread of all the techniques discussed or just one or two? If you are restricting yourself to one or two then is it possible that you are restricting your potential?

REFINING YOUR GOALS

Just as work priorities keep changing, so will personal development priorities. Suddenly some skills become urgent (perhaps in preparation for an interview), whilst others can disappear equally as quickly (after getting a new job). What is essential is that the goals you set are always current. Therefore they need constant revisiting and updating.

During this process it is timely to consider whether your goals can be refined into being more specific, or more targeted. You will have worked with your goals over a period of time. Some will have been achieved, others will have been superseded by time. They now have to be more focused and reduced in number.

> **Refining your goals to the top three will enable them to be remembered more easily and targeted more specifically towards your personal success.**

USING THE POWER OF OTHERS

As mentioned earlier, people are a very valuable resource in your development. They hold the key to the information you require and more importantly they know other people. They can recommend people to you and you to others, so when you communicate with one person, you are actually sending out communication lines with many others.

Some people are undoubtedly more powerful than others, but why is that so? Is it something we bestow upon them because we know of their connections, something the organisation bestows upon them as a representation of their position, or is it something they themselves have assumed?

Understanding the sources of power
Individual power stems from one or more of five factors:

1. **Expert** knowledge or skill. Others may need this skill or value it, and therefore any person possessing this will have considerable power within the organisation. A diminishing need for the skill also corresponds with diminishing power.

2. **Authority** delegated to the individual, often in the form of a formal position, impressive job title, own office, large budget, high level decision making, *etc*. Others in the organisation may be in awe of this person; however demotion or a sideways move to a marginalised position can profoundly diminish this power.

3. **Reward** power, or those who have the ability to grant rewards to others. This may be in the form of additional pay, the control of 'perks', or the assignment of tasks.

4. **Coercive** power, or those who have the ability to penalise others. This may range from a possible dismissal to a withdrawal of friendship.

5. **Charismatic** power of those who are noticed immediately. It is often said that they have a 'presence'. Their personality is such that they draw people to them and others are willing to be led.

Think of any powerful people you know. What types of power do they have or use?

Being part of a powerful group
Being part of a group or on a project team can give you power of a different kind. This is a collective power which is shared by all the group members. For a group or team to have this power it needs to have some combination of the following:

● play a significant role in major organisational decision processes

- deal with uncertainty faced by the organisation, for example a reorganisation or change project which involves forecasting and assessing risks

- control the supply of essential resources to the organisation

- control the methods of communication throughout the organisation

- be a pivotal part in one or two key operations.

If you have been part of a central team, reflect back on the power that the team enjoyed during the project. What happened after the project? It is likely that the power diminished in time.

INCORPORATING YOUR NEW SKILLS INTO WORK

It is within the workplace that you will be practising your new skills. Successfully integrating these skills into your job will ensure that you are more effective and efficient. Attaining new skills not only enables you to do a job better, it also broadens the mind and helps you think differently about other tasks. For example, once a person has gained computer skills and feels comfortable with them, they will start to look at other aspects of their job that can be computerised. They would not have thought this way before. In a similar way, after reading and practising communication skills, a person is more likely to extend this thinking to all communication mechanisms within his or her department. So the effects can be far reaching – a little knowledge can go a long way.

GETTING NOTICED

Getting noticed is essential. However, getting noticed in the right way is the key. People make major decisions based on very little factual information. Frighteningly, research shows that others make a decision about our personality and ability before we open our mouths, based purely on our looks.

As creatures of habit we are more likely to employ or promote people we know, in some instances rather a case of 'better the devil you know than the devil you don't'. It therefore pays for you to be noticed and get known. You need to be on greeting terms with as many major players in your organisation and any sister organisations as possible.

Being visible

Not everyone welcomes attention but to move up that career ladder you need to be visible. That does not mean being the loudest or the most noticed person in the room, but it does mean being in the right place at the right time and in the right company. Networking or being in a mentoring relationship with a senior manager is good, but lunching with them publicly can be better.

It may be despised by others but being seen with the right people matters. It implies that you are in their team, on their level, or part of their 'set'. When being interviewed for a senior post (that you don't expect to get) rejoice that you made the shortlist for interview. People start to see you as having that calibre and therefore being a definite contender for any future senior roles.

Think about which are the most important meetings or gatherings, and try to be there. Even if you are only holding your manager's notes! People there will see you and assume you are there for other reasons. Always attend leaving and Christmas functions. Mingle and talk to as many people as possible. Once you have been labelled 'someone who is going somewhere' there is very little to stop you achieving it.

Assuming the role

Visual perceptions can confuse and fool. When you mix with senior managers at a conference, other delegates assume you are also of that level. People make great assumptions based on very little evidence. For this reason never turn down the opportunity to stand-in for your manager at a meeting or on a course.

Have you ever been to an event and noticed someone there whose name and occupation you didn't know, but they had an air of importance, and therefore you assumed they were important?

In developing your skills it is important to develop your sense of **you**. You may have put many hours into gaining management skills, but do you walk tall and look confident? Or do you slope around hoping no one will notice you? – because that is what will happen when it is promotion time. It does not matter at what level you are currently – you need to assume the bearing and gestures of your next move up the career ladder.

When interviewing candidates for a new job, the recruitment team will want to be assured that the person they select can do the job, not grow into it. Therefore you need to be one step ahead and present a picture of a confident individual who is capable not only of their current role but also that of the one above. They need visual confirmation of what your skills portfolio is telling them, not conflicting information. It also makes the decision easier for the recruitment team. They do not have to probe into why a person's portfolio does not appear to match their appearance or demeanour. This would set up conflict in their minds and they may feel that probing is not worth the effort, especially if there is another candidate who already matches their expectations.

Dressing the part

Dressing for the role you want is also essential, as general appearance is still noted far more than one would think. Many books have been written on creating the right impression, but most are embellishments of the following rules:

● Buy one good quality suit in a neutral colour. Use as many blouses, shirts, ties and scarves as you like, using the colour combinations and patterns to express your personality. There is no need for 'good' dressing to be dull or unfashionable.

● Make sure your shoes are always clean and well maintained. Socks should match suit colour and tights should be subdued colours.

● Ensure your personal grooming leaves you with a neat appearance: no birds' nest hair or uneven shaving. Don't use too much make-up, perfume or jewellery.

TIP – look up the organisational ladder at someone you admire – how they dress will give you a clue as to how to dress for success.

If you are working in an industrial environment then it is important that you dress for the job. Wearing a suit whilst undertaking industrial work would be inappropriate and look ridiculous.

USING STRONGER TECHNIQUES

This section is aimed at people who feel totally comfortable with their development so far and would like to make a greater impression. As with all of these techniques there is a risk attached. In this case the main risk is that overconfidence can be one step away from pushiness or over-familiarity, which would make you most unpopular. Contain the urge to over promote yourself and your endeavours will be rewarded.

Opportunity knocks

Never let an opportunity pass. Be on the look-out for them all the time and grab them with both hands when they occur. If you enjoyed a seminar and thought the speaker the type of person you should know, then introduce yourself at the end, even if it means waiting behind a line of others. Be bold and make an impact, you may never get this opportunity again and would spend the remainder of the day kicking yourself if you allowed it to slip by.

If you overhear someone discussing an interesting project which will soon arise do not be afraid to interrupt them and say, 'I apologise for being rude but I could not help overhear you discussing the new project. Do you know when they are likely to be selecting the team for it?' They may be able to tell you, they may not, but it is also another opportunity for introducing yourself and making an impression.

Taking advantage of opportunities is not always easy, especially if you are naturally shy. However, how often have you heard others say, 'I should have approached them, I've wished a million times that I had'. Don't wish your life away, **do it now**!

Seek and ye shall find

Proactively seeking out people you know have influence is also another technique to push yourself ahead. It takes investment time to sit down and analyse the organisation and pinpoint who within it is able to promote your career. Although this is something that we don't always like to do: we like to think that we just come across people who happen to be able to help us. Well, sometimes that does happen but how long have you got to wait? Do you have time to lurk in the executive corridor for long stretches, hoping to be noticed? I don't think so.

You need to target people both inside and outside your organisation, a 'hit list' if you like. Make a list of people you will want to approach, whom you know will be able to help you succeed. Now think, where can they be found?

Contriving an introduction

Finding out where people can be found is more difficult than contriving an introduction. When located, the simplest method is to walk straight up and introduce yourself, but it is difficult to then take the conversation anywhere else. It is so much simpler if you meet at a tennis club or some other sporting venue where you can be introduced by a third party and immediately you have a subject for discussion – 'Would you be interested in a game sometime?' If you are not sure where they can be found, then ask around. It is highly likely that the people who work for this person will know their hobbies and habits. It may even be as easy as 'He always eats in the staff restaurant at 12.30 each day', in which case make sure you are there at the same time and ask if you can share his table.

Contriving an introduction is not cheating – it is just speeding-up the introduction you hoped would happen in the fullness of time. If you saw someone you considered attractive you would not think twice about planning a way to meet. This is the same principle and equally concerns your future, but with a different outcome!

CASE STUDIES

Richard's powerful quest

Richard decides to take a closer look at power and how it is distributed and used in his organisation. He has never thought of different types of power before and wants to put his theories to the test. He is intrigued by the findings and decides to stretch them further by involving senior management. He has interested certain parties enough to be invited to present his thoughts at the next senior management meeting. Although he is a bit nervous of presentation, Richard decides this is an opportunity too big to refuse and so he goes in with a list of positive outcomes he wants from the meeting.

Carol feels the part

Carol decides that she wants to increase her visibility. She wants to be seen and heard in the right places. Her mentor has taken her along to a few meetings and on each occasion she has planned her clothes very carefully. For her birthday, her husband has bought her a leather briefcase and, at Christmas, a matching leather diary/notebook. Carol is now starting to feel as good as she looks. Carol has her eye on a vacancy which has just arisen in the personnel department and is keen to let people know she should be considered a serious candidate for the position.

Dean's dressing down

Dean is keen to dress for his future but the problem is that all his colleagues dress down and wear trainers. He is worried that not only will his colleagues think a sudden, dramatic change in dress is a bit strange, but also that if he wears a suit he will no longer be dressing like them. He thinks they might make fun of him or even ostracise him. He discusses his concerns at length with his coach. She advises him to not move straight from his current casual dress to a sharp suit, and suggests that he takes a more gentle change over a longer time period. To start with, perhaps, change the shoes to a smart but casual leather pair – perhaps some loafers. Then after a couple of weeks, change his current black trousers for a smarter pair with a better cut. The important thing is to make the change gradually. Dean feels happy with this advice and decides to give it a go.

POINTS TO CONSIDER

1. Make a list of the techniques you are using. If there are only one or two consider why this is. Are you unsure of the others, do you feel comfortable with them?

2. Make sure you are noticed by organising a presentation in front of a group of people. It could be a team briefing or describing a project you are on to a different group of managers.

3. Revisit the different types of power people have. Who do you know who uses this type of power in each category (they may have more than one)? Do you have any of these types of power?

9
Reaching Out

Self development and increasing your skills can be infectious – others will want to copy you. Reach out and share your ideas with them. One facet of self development is the development of others. If you have found something good that works for you, then it should be shared so that others (and the organisation) may benefit.

PASSING YOUR KNOWLEDGE ON TO OTHERS

As your confidence increases others will notice a change. When a move or promotion is in the offing then your accomplishments will be even more obvious and overtly discussed by colleagues. This is natural as they will wonder at your meteoric rise and try to work out how you managed to get yourself on the fast track. You may be feeling a little more confident but otherwise unchanged, so how can you check that you are 'growing' in your learning? You:

● are in control of the process surrounding you

● take a more active role in discussions around you

● invite others to give you direct and active feedback based on your performance, and act on it

● behave as though you are on a long journey of discovery rather than as if you have arrived and are now bored

● show greater awareness of your needs and do not mind pushing to ensure they are met

● create a climate of curiosity, challenge and questioning wherever you go

● provide feedback to others and encourage ways for them to learn.

Don't be shy. These are the signs that you feel confident in your current job and are, perhaps, ready for a greater challenge.

Good news should always be shared. There are many ways that you could do this, but some are suggested below.

Becoming a mentor or coach

Just as you have relied on the experience of a mentor or coach it may be that, in time, you are asked to fulfil this function on behalf of another. If your organisation already supports a mentoring/coaching facility, you may decide to volunteer to become a mentor/coach, using your experience from 'the other side' to help you through.

Becoming a mentor or coach to another individual can be a most rewarding experience and one where you are able to 'give back' some of the time others invested in you. It is difficult to quantify the sheer pleasure one can get from seeing others succeed, especially knowing that you have played a great part in that success.

Starting a development 'club'

Start up a development club in your organisation. In the same way that special interest groups form to discuss certain topics, your group can discuss the merits (or otherwise) of different types of learning and development. In fact you could use the techniques found in this book to help you set agendas, and develop a group portfolio. Here are some other ideas:

● Invite someone from the training department to talk about what is on offer within the organisation.

● Invite a representative from your local college to discuss the courses they offer and any subsidised funding arrangements.

● Have a 'development opportunity of the month' and hold a full discussion around whether this would work in your organisation and where there are problems.

● Invite a coaching professional to discuss how they see coaching and what they do for you.

Remember – teams or groups hold their own type of power and can influence the organisation. Your development club could help shape or influence the future of training within your organisation.

Passing your experience on to the training/personnel department

Approach your training or personnel officer to discuss how your approach to personal development could be experienced by all. Share your ideas on the development opportunities you have used and ask how these could be disseminated to a wider audience. It is likely that they will be impressed by your enthusiasm, and may use you as a guest speaker on one of their courses. Possibly they are thinking of introducing something along those lines into the organisation, and need an ally, or someone who has experienced this at close range, to speak to managers.

Speaking about your experience

If you are asked to speak publicly about your experience in self development, then take this as another chance to add skills to your portfolio. It may be that you are asked to present to your management team, give a presentation to a project team, or even to a meeting of an institute which is anxious to promote continuous professional development (CPD). Whatever the situation, be confident that you are talking about one of the hottest subjects today – and one that many people will want to hear about.

Some people have always taken a lead in their career progression, but never before have so many organisations given direct encouragement. With redundancies and downsizing, people are feeling insecure and need to gain some sort of control over their future. In speaking about your experience you will be able to offer them that security – security born from the knowledge that you control your own destiny, and that the power to make things happen is in your hands alone.

When you speak you will be addressing many people and consequently be in a very powerful position. Use that power to push your message across and become a person of influence, someone who is remembered.

Sharing the secret with your manager

When you are next in an appraisal, or discussing your career with your manager, tell them the secret of your planned development. They will be impressed at how much thought and work you have put into this. They may even be able to help with some more suggestions. If you have the opportunity you might also like to share your portfolio. It will demonstrate how your planning has progressed and will allow them to see the direction in which you are moving. If your manager wants to extend some of your experience to the others in the department, then welcome it. Often people worry that others will catch up on them in the development stakes, but if you are truly confident in your development then this will not cause you a problem.

INFLUENCING COLLEAGUES

When colleagues see the effects of your self development they will be impressed, but may not recognise the considerable dedication required. This dedication does not come without a price and not everyone is willing to pay. There will always be people who are not willing to put in the time, but want the rewards nonetheless.

> **Self development is one area where if there is no input there will be no output.**

However, influencing skills can be brought into play to persuade colleagues what we already know – that if we don't hone the skills required by the organisation of the future, then we will be unemployed. If we do take the time to learn and practise those skills, then our value will rise.

Warning – if others do not want to develop their skills, do not make yourself unpopular by placing undue pressure on them. There will always be those who are content to bumble along and take their chances. Leave them to it and fly alone!

Influencing downwards

If you are in a position of authority, your staff will notice your change of approach. You are in an excellent position to introduce them to a whole range of self development techniques. Annual appraisals are an ideal time for discussing future opportunities within their career structure and simply asking, 'Where do you intend to be in five years' time?', and 'How do you plan to get there?'

If appraisals are many months away then development opportunities can be discussed at team meetings. Make it a team rule that from now on every time one of the team attends a training course or a seminar, they are duty bound to provide the remainder of the team with a presentation or overview of the topic and relevant learning points and outcomes. This will enhance their powers of presentation *and* present a learning opportunity for the remainder of the team. It will also be very evident from the spread of presentations, which team members are taking advantages of the training opportunities, and which are not.

Even if you are not in a position of line managing staff do not be surprised if you are still approached by other junior members of staff. It is so easy to forget that others watch us constantly. People we do not know hold us in high esteem, and watch our career progress – and we don't even know about it. Be a role model for those lower grades and welcome any approach.

Influencing upwards

It is not often that people think of influencing *up* the organisation. We hold onto a belief that those in the hierarchy above us are there to nurture us and know best. It can come as a surprise that, as you rise in stature, you start to notice the shortcomings of those above.

While managers are developing their staff, who develops the managers? Senior managers have development needs too and are often forgotten. They need the skills to steer the boat (the organisation) through the choppy seas of change, and deal with the ailing crew and create a positive atmosphere to see you all through to the next port, by which time the galleon might have metamorphosed into an ocean liner with several tug boats.

Suggesting to senior management that they may have skills needs and require coaching support is not easy. For a start how do you approach these people? Senior managers do not have time to attend more meetings so use a communication channel already available, for example one of their management team meetings. You would need to approach the chair in advance to negotiate a 'slot' on the agenda to present a short introduction to self development. It could describe some of the methods discussed in this book, focus on your experience, and then end with an open question around their own development needs which could be left for discussion. Alternatively introduce the subject with your personnel or training officer who will be able to provide the company perspective. It may be that as part of your development (again) you help organise or plan a programme.

Influencing across

Influencing colleagues may seem an easier option but it is beset with its own problems. Colleagues have their own agendas which are unknown to you. Their opinions of you will differ and that will influence their decisions regarding your ideas. Do not be surprised if colleagues shout down your ideas in the first instance – they may be jealous or have hidden fears around your and their achievement. Not everyone wants to climb to the top of the tree, and it would be a very top-heavy tree if they were all able to do so.

Try introducing self development ideas within team discussions. It may be that you think two members of staff would benefit from learning each other's jobs, or from workshadowing another member of staff to gain an insight to another role. On a simpler level you might want to start a discussion on whether, as a team, you want to be multi-functional (each member be able to do several jobs) or specialist (each member has their own job). You do not have to be the team leader to suggest adding a discussion to the agenda, and some interesting points may come out of it.

The real 'key' to influencing your colleagues is to display your pride in your own development. As they see you in action, and the positive results, they will either want to join you or indicate that they don't share your dedication. If it is the former, then rejoice in sharing your ideas, if it is the latter then never push. It may not be the right time in their careers to make this decision.

PUSHING THE POWER UP THE ORGANISATION

Many organisations are historic in the way they operate. They too are struggling with this new way of working. Some bureaucratic organisational structures do not support matrix style management where line management and authority may lie with different individuals for different projects. They are also struggling with the new ways that people work, the end of the traditional 9 to 5 working day, flexible working, and the loss of the traditional weekend. Perhaps it is up to you to push your power up the organisation and inform senior management what a change in approach to learning can do.

Harnessing the power

Organisations are not buildings or structures, they are made of people, individual people who all have unique knowledge and information. The power of that information is slowly being recognised. From an organisational point of view, when mass redundancies are implemented it is knowledge and experience that are walking out of the door. Organisations which made huge redundancies when re-engineering in the 1980s experienced a 'brain drain' afterwards. Information can be captured but skills, knowledge and experience, which formed the earlier culture, will be gone. Therefore developing your skills increases your worth.

Forward thinking organisations are now realising this and are designing ways of harnessing information and recording it in some way. They realise that in the new way of working where staff come and go (often to the highest bidder) the organisation without a pool of knowledge and experience is left wanting.

Enhancing the information flow

For this concept to be accepted and carried through it needs to be placed at a strategic level so that it infiltrates every aspect and layer of the organisation. It is only when acceptance of this concept is at a high level that information will begin to flow more readily throughout the organisation. One way of kick starting information flow would be to start a simple database containing the names and details of any areas of major study undertaken by individuals within the organisation. For the individual, this may mean filling in a form upon commencing or completing their area of study, which could then be input into the system. Anyone wanting to tap into any specialist skills at a later date could search the database on that subject or any allied skills.

Initially a project of this type would need a directive to ensure that all staff submitted their skills areas. However, in time the information would be so useful that it would become part of the culture of the organisation and become integrated into daily activities. Eventually it will be merely 'something we do round here'.

Getting top management to take the lead on development is not easy, but worth pursuing. When they see the power behind sharing organisational knowledge, and the lead it gives them over their competitors, they will become enthused and keen to participate.

USING OTHERS TO DEVELOP YOURSELF FURTHER

There are a number of ways in which people can help you to develop – mentoring and coaching (Chapter 6) are just two ways already explored. Through people you will:

● increase your visibility

● meet other people

● communicate with a wider audience.

Explaining secondments

A secondment is when you take time out from your current role to try something new, often working in a different role. It could be any length of time, two weeks or two years, and it may not be full time. It is not unknown to be seconded to a project for three days a week over a period of six months.

Secondments are an excellent way of:

● experiencing a different role

● exploring new ways of working

● exploring a different organisation

● meeting new contacts

● working in a different way.

Secondments may be initiated by any member of staff but need line management approval. The best way of securing a secondment is to make a business case to your manager explaining:

1. Why you want a secondment.

2. Why this particular secondment opportunity is attractive.

3. What you hope to gain from the experience.

4. What the organisation will gain from the experience.

5. How long you would be away.

6. How your work would be covered in your absence.

7. How you would manage your return to the workplace.

8. How you would integrate the learning into your job.

All secondments carry risks. There is the risk on the employer's side that you will not return (or return only to leave shortly after), and the risk on your side that your position may not be kept open for you (or that the person replacing you for the duration of the secondment is more efficient or effective). These risks can be overcome through the careful planning of the eight points above together with either a letter of understanding or 'contract' drawn up between manager and employee.

Workshadowing and observing
Workshadowing is a technique where one person follows, or 'shadows', another person, watching how they spend their typical day. It is a technique you should consider if you are interested in a particular job and

would like to see how that job is carried out 'warts and all'. It can also be a good way of observing in action someone you professionally admire.

Following someone around for a few days can be difficult. Firstly there is the discomfort factor, by both the observer and the observed. It is not easy being watched, nor is it easy, surprisingly, watching someone else. Secondly there is the logistics of not being able to dash off to a meeting without taking someone else along. Not everyone has their own comfortable office, therefore having to share workspace with someone else, even for a few days, can be uncomfortable. Lastly there is the inability to shorten any discussion to 'in-speak'. Often when two people are talking about a subject known to them, they will shorten their speech to acronyms and in-house jargon. If there is another person present, everything has to be explained to the third party, which interrupts flow and can make negotiating difficult.

Contracting

Taking a decision to pursue contract work is not easy. Gone are the regular pay days and the promotion prospects. There are no opportunities to join the staff club or go on staff trips. Of course it may not be a personal decision to try contracting. Often it is the first port of call for people who have been made redundant.

Contracting is often given bad press, but it is actually an excellent way of:

● trying out new organisations

● trying out different jobs

● getting used to being mobile

● gaining confidence in your abilities

● learning new systems/software/technology

● meeting lots of new people.

If you are ever in a position to try contract work, give it 100 per cent. Many people find that they get hooked on the idea of working on short-term projects, where they can move on and leave the organisation behind. It is an easy situation which suits both parties and can quite often pay higher than a regular salary, especially for specialist skills.

SETTING UP NETWORKS

Although networking has been around for a long time, it has been mainly confined to the 'old boy network', using one's contacts to gain jobs
and contracts. Although still in evidence today, new types of networking
have emerged. This new networking allows the formation of a formal
network, from scratch, with people who do not necessarily know each
other. The only thing they have in common is a special interest, skill, or
just the need to mix with a certain group. Informal networking can be
just keeping in-touch with like-minded people. Quite often after a training event, people are invited to spend some time 'networking', which
can mean simply exchanging business cards.

Creating a new network

When considering creating a network for the first time the objective
must be clear. Ask yourself the following questions:

1. Why should people (often in their spare time) want to meet others?

2. What will their expectations be?

3. Are these expectations likely to be achieved?

4. Is the network able to stand alone or is it a bolt-on to a presentation
    or open discussion?

Once the objective is clear the rules need to be considered. Use the
following questions as a prompt:

1. How will people hear about the network?

2. How will people join the network (invitation only/free for all)?

3. Will anyone be barred from joining the network?

4. What will be the maximum number of members?

5. How will the network be managed?

6. How regularly will it meet?

Talking this a step further, the housekeeping also needs thought:

1. Where will the network be held (venue)?

2. What time of day will it meet?

3. For how long will it meet?

4. Will there be refreshments?

When you have firm answers to the above issues, they can be formulated into a proposal. With this proposal you will be able to approach senior management through whichever route is most suitable, line manager or personnel department. It may be that the proposal is not for your organisation, but perhaps for an institute or outside 'body', in which case they can be approached direct.

Selling the network
Using the approach outlined above, you will be able to use your proposal as a powerful persuasive tool. However, the idea will still need 'selling'.
Selling the network is on two levels:

1. To the organisation/institute/authoritative body.

2. To the people intending to use it.

Approaching the organisation/institute/authoritative body
When you are ready to sell your idea, the first approach is often most effective by phone. Outline the idea for your network and at the same time ask whether you may send your written proposal. Attach a letter (or internal memo), similar to the one shown in Figure 12, to the proposal, requesting a follow up call or visit in a few days' time. After a few days, by which time the proposal will have been considered, phone to either discuss or make an appointment to visit.

Getting people to join the network
Networks mostly sell themselves once they are up and running but they need an initial 'push' to help them on their way.
If the network is internal to the organisation, it could be advertised through the company magazine or intranet. This will afford it the highest saturation and ensure it reaches the attention of most of the staff. However, the network may not be targeted at all staff and therefore it may not be appropriate to advertise it so widely. It may be that it is only of interest to individuals on a management programme, with a specific

MEMO

From: Emma Pavitt

To: Mr Jenkins

Subject: Internal Network Report

Date: 30th September 199X

I contacted you recently concerning the introduction of an official network within the organisation. I enclose my report outlining how the network would operate and the benefits to both the organisation and individuals from participating.

I will contact you again in a few days' time for your initial comments, and then at the same time I can make an appointment with you to discuss the proposal in greater depth.

Fig. 12. Sample networking memo.

skill, or of a certain grade. If this is the case then it becomes more important to reach the right people. The more narrow the criteria, the fewer people it will attract. Bear in mind that you will need a minimum number for the network to function.

If there is an associated training programme, you could contact the trainer or facilitator and request a ten minute slot to advertise the network. This is an excellent way of reaching a whole group of people who might need support.

Once networks are established, they are often kept rolling by faithful individuals bringing 'guests' with them. Guests can swell numbers and, if from a different organisation, can offer a fresh perspective. For that reason they could form an important part of your sales proposal which will incorporate the future of the network. It may not be appropriate for guests to be invited, especially if the criteria are stringent. In this instance it becomes more important than ever to keep the network alive and fresh so the numbers do not drop.

CASE STUDIES

Richard shares his experience

Richard likes being a mentor. He enjoys imparting his vast experience and also the lively conversations they have. Richard feels that many of his colleagues would benefit from this experience too. He also thinks that his organisation would benefit considerably. He decides to speak with the training department and then present his idea of a fully supported mentoring programme to senior management following the success of his last presentation. He knows that his colleagues may view his enthusiasm as out of character with the 'old Richard', but the 'new Richard' is confident in taking his bold ideas higher if necessary, such is his conviction.

Carol starts a club

Carol decides to start a development club during her lunchtimes. It will meet only once a month and she already has a year's worth of agenda items. She contacts the personnel and training department to see if there are any objections, but there appears to be none, so she shows her ideas to her line manager. Although she is keen on pursuing the vacancy in the personnel department, she feels that if she is unsuccessful, then she is still developing herself in that general direction through the club. Carol is very clear who her club is aimed at (who the customer will be) and she designs posters on her computer which she hopes will attract the right people. She has given her number as a contact for more information, and now she is poised for that first call.

Dean gets a network going

Dean cannot find the kind of network which excites him. He thinks therefore that there must be lots of other young people who also feel the same way. He thinks that perhaps he can do something interesting and different. He decides to use the Internet to set up a web page and monitor or communicate with those who visit its site. After a good response he hires a room in a local hotel, advertises on his web site, and produces flyers which he sends to all the computer companies he knows nearby – and waits with anticipation on the first night.

POINTS TO CONSIDER

1. Find out whether any papers or reports have been submitted to senior management about harnessing the power of information within your organisation.

2. Look at your colleagues and identify who is driven and ambitious. Think about approaching them.

3. Identify or locate a network that would interest you.

10
Reflecting on Experiences

The most important part of all development is reflecting on experiences. In the same way that it is all too easy to skip the highly recommended stretching out and cooling down period after an active workout, it is easy to skip the reflection phase – especially if it means reliving a painful or embarrassing experience.

REVISITING THE ACTION PLAN

It is only through reflection that experience can be put in perspective. Research has shown that people remember their mistakes for years after the event, while others involved at the time (unless the mistake had a profound effect on them) forget the issue fairly soon afterwards. Unfortunately, holding onto the memory is self punishing and will not allow the individual to move on past the event. They will be caught in a constant cycle of anger and hurt. To enable the person to move forward, these negative feelings must be allowed to go while the positive learning from the event remains. This technique of mapping positive experiences over negative ones enables the individual to accept the situation, move forward, and grow.

In fact many people would argue that true leaning should not *end* with reflection but *start* with reflection.

**It is only when reflecting today that we see
our needs for tomorrow.**

Starting your revisal

Turn to your portfolio, particularly your action plan. Look at your revised goals and the progress you have made. Is it time to reflect formally on what you have learnt? Quite often unidentified additional learning emerges which was not the original intention of an exercise. For

Reflective Log

Course/Activity Title

Date

Brief account of the activity

Which skills areas were covered by this activity?

What were your conclusions?

What further action is required?

How will this be reflected in your future planning?

Fig. 13. Reflective log.

example, a secondment to another organisation to perform a project may have resulted in an introduction to a network whose members have proved most useful. The secondment arrangement should already be in your portfolio, but the details of the network and any emerging contacts will not be. This information should also be captured formally for inclusion in your portfolio.

There may also be occasions when you have attended a course and need to capture your thoughts on the event. A reflective log on this can be very helpful. Completing it is like writing a diary and requires an equal amount of self discipline, albeit less frequently.

Figure 13 shows an example of a reflective log. Think about completing one at least once a year based on your review of your action plan, and additional ones following any courses attended during the year.

COPING WITH FEEDBACK

Everyone needs feedback to enable them to improve on their performance. It can feel great to receive positive feedback, but the reverse is also true. Feedback which exposes a lack of skills can be difficult to accept. Often, non-acceptance manifests itself as anger or embarrassment. Learning to accept feedback, whether positive or negative, is a very important factor in self development.

Your willingness to seek feedback will also be noticed by your managers. It is far easier to accept that you were unsuccessful in getting that job or promotion and then slink away, than to return to ask why. Through your interest in feedback you are demonstrating your commitment towards getting it right next time. Of course taking action on that feedback is up to you.

The table below demonstrates how the advantages of seeking feedback far outweigh the disadvantages.

Advantages	Disadvantages
You will gain valuable information.	It may be embarrassing to be told negative things.
The person providing the feedback may point you in some interesting directions to help you in your development.	The person providing the feedback may not value something you are promoting as a strength.
Inviting feedback is seen as a positive step by most people.	Not being able to accept feedback is seen as an additional negative skill by many.

Putting it all in perspective

When seeking feedback it is important to remember that it is subjective. That means the feedback you receive will depend on the thoughts and views of the person providing it. It is therefore little value if you do not respect that person's judgement.

It is also valid only for that one occasion on which it is based. For example, the feedback you receive on one job application will not be applicable to others where the skills requirement is different.

Listen to feedback, hear what is being said and then consider whether you agree with the comments. If you accept the feedback, you will be able to take corrective action; if not, then talk the issue through with someone whose views and advice you respect, possibly your mentor.

REWARDING THE EXPERIENCE

Being disciplined enough to grasp and move forward in your own development deserves reward. Hopefully much of that reward will come in the form of praise from your manager, increased salary and/or promotion.

Whether or not this is the case, take some time out to reward yourself personally. Book a meal in a good restaurant, buy a bottle of champagne, a new suit, or a box of chocolates. Whatever fits your lifestyle and/or your pocket.

As mentioned earlier, taking time out to celebrate success is crucial. At the time it may seem that there is not sufficient space in your diary or that it was really not such a big deal, but every success should be celebrated and made to feel special. It is by celebrating these successes that we are producing our own tempting 'carrot' to continue onwards. How often have you celebrated in select surroundings, for example a fine restaurant, only to think 'I would love the excuse to do this again'? Then make that memory your personal 'carrot' for carrying the development forward. Make a promise that you will relive the experience when you achieve that pay rise, or promotion. Then make sure you do it!

PLANNING FOR THE FUTURE

Planning must continue. With greater goals in front and a wealth of experience behind there is only one way – and that is forward. However, just as planning played a large part in deciding what skills you required in the beginning, it is planning once more that will push you forward.

'In preparing for battle, I have always found that plans are useless but planning is indispensable.'

Dwight D Eisenhower

Jobs change, situations change, you change, but rather than make that an excuse not to plan, realise that it is a greater reinforcement for planning ahead. Without a plan you will go nowhere. The skills you have worked so hard to achieve will become outdated. Remember – if you don't use it, you lose it.

Complacency is the enemy of planning. Feeling that you have arrived is a temporary state and to move any further forward we have to plan one step ahead. You need to be looking to broaden your skills portfolio rather than sitting back on what you have achieved. Celebrate success, yes, but don't let the party go on too long.

Creating your CPD

Continuous Professional Development (CPD) is the name given to the continuous career-linked quest for development. Many institutes promote CPD and may remove membership if proof of it is not forthcoming in the form of a career plan and/or portfolio. The reason for this is not to make members jump through hoops to maintain membership but to ensure professional learning is current.

'One thing only that I know, and that is that I know nothing.'

Socrates

Learning is an ongoing quest. Look back at the learning ring (Figure 6). Learning is cyclical and therefore a continuous process. From the experience comes not only understanding but a need to know something else or to further the learning in some way. Most organisations make the provision for their employees to learn, particularly those skills which contribute towards the 'bottom line' of the business. The individual's job and working environment will present challenges or new issues which must be dealt with. Meeting those challenges, learning from them, using new knowledge, skills and understanding, that is the essence of CPD.

In some instances, to maintain membership of an institute, CPD needs to be collected and presented in some way. The portfolio described throughout this book is an excellent way of verifying your CPD. It will provide them with a full account of your development in an organised and easy-to-understand way. Proof of CPD may also be requested at interviews as this becomes an essential, competitive criterion for a fast track career of the future.

SPREADING THE NEWS

When something has worked for you, you automatically want to spread the news. As part of your reflection, ask yourself which techniques have worked so well for you that you would like to share that information with everyone else. When you have done this, write a piece for your internal magazine, newsheet or intranet. Explain:

● what made you consider self development

● how you took it forward

● the methods/techniques used

● how you recorded your progress

● the results achieved.

Complete the article with a section thanking people for their help and support and leave contact details in case someone wants to follow up with an enquiry.

Writing about your experience for a professional journal is also a good way of spreading the news and at the same time producing evidence of your development. Good articles are always welcome by journals, especially if they have a current or futuristic theme or feel. We cannot always predict the future but we like reading about it, especially if that reading allays some of our fears, such as unemployment.

Publications often require a 'bio-pic' if they decide to feature someone who has completed a project or gained promotion. This just means a paragraph or two about the person, their career to date and how they achieved success. This is another point at which you can spread the news about self development opportunities and how they have helped you.

CASE STUDIES

Richard feels the benefits

Richard was not seeking promotion, he just wanted to remain employed. He has continued to do so and senior management are very interested in his mentoring programme and views on self development. They cannot understand why they have not noticed him before. However, the biggest change for Richard is that he no longer fears redundancy and this shows in his general confidence. He is finding the charity work hugely rewarding. He feels that if he were ever to lose his local government job he would maintain continuity and gain satisfaction from his charity work. This makes Richard far more comfortable about facing the future, and has a positive effect on his family too.

Carol gets her break

Carol is thrilled when she is offered the job in personnel. However, she still approaches her interviewers for feedback. She wants to know why they offered her the job so that she can be aware of the skills they were seeking. Her feedback lists her enthusiasm, office skills, general appearance, the mentoring she has undertaken and also includes her development club. They were also impressed with the portfolio she took along to the interview. Carol decides to go out to celebrate, but knows that as soon as she is settled in her new position she must return to her portfolio to plan her next year.

Dean takes stock

Dean's network is a great success. He has opened up his field of contacts considerably. At one event he is approached by a member of staff from a competitive organisation who invites Dean to visit and share his technical knowledge and views with some members of his project team. Dean accepts and so impresses the team that he is offered a job within the new organisation, at a higher salary. Unbeknown to Dean, his girlfriend, Sarah, has been secretly working on a portfolio at the same time as helping Dean. She has impressed her employers at the travel agency and had been taken on full time in addition to starting a course of NVQ training. Their future prospects suddenly look brighter.

POINTS TO CONSIDER

1. Complete a reflective log after a course or reading a book.

2. Prepare a 'bio-pic' about yourself and keep it in your portfolio.

3. Think of three ways in which you could thank people for the support they have given you.

Glossary

Action plan. A structured set of related items which describe the options for taking learning forward to meet the specified goals.

Acronyms. The initial letter of frequently-used phrases, for example, CPD.

Attitude. Type of behaviour indicating opinions – can be demonstrated through the way you react to situations.

Audit. An inspection process for reviewing an item and determining its value.

Brain drain. The loss of knowledge when large numbers of knowledgeable staff leave the organisation.

Coach. A person who uses coaching skills to advise you and increase your performance.

Competence. Ability to meet certain criteria.

Contingency planning. Planning for recovery from disasters, mistakes or failure to meet targets.

CPD. Continuous Professional Development – a method of ensuring your professional knowledge is current.

Creative thinking. Exploring radical ways of solving problems or creating new ideas.

Culture. The way in which an organisation undertakes actions or develops processes, quite simply it is 'the way things are done around here'.

CV. Curriculum vitae, a written record of your working history.

Distance learning. A form of learning using materials which have been designed to be used away from the traditional training environment, or in the learner's own time.

Downsizing. A reduction in the number of the workforce.

Evaluation. A process to decide whether the objectives of the task have been met.

Experiential skills. Skills emanating from life experiences.

Facilitator. A person who guides the group to enable learning to take place.

Flexible working. A less structured way of working which may involve working from different bases, teleworking, hot-desking, variable hours *etc*.

Goal. The desired end result, the overall objective.

Innovators. People who create original new ideas or processes.

International managing. A new style of managing where the team may be multi-national or the manager controls teams across the world. It requires skills and knowledge in different cultures.

Internet. The World Wide Web, a global communication and information highway.

Intranet. An advanced internal communication mechanism using networked computers.

Learning organisation. An organisation that is willing to learn and to encourage their staff to contribute to that learning.

Life experiences. The experiences gained from life situations.

Mental agility. The ability to think quickly, often flicking between a number of subjects.

Mentor. A wise person.

Mind Map®. A thought generation and organisation technique originated by Tony Buzan to stimulate and capture creative thought processes.

Motivation. The reason for undertaking certain actions.

Networking. Mixing with a group of people with a view to making contacts or increasing information.

NVQ. National Vocational Qualifications – qualifications that test competence in a skill.

Personal motivation factor. The personal reason you have for undertaking an action.

Portfolio. An amassed record of your learning.

Psychometric tests. Tests which classify according to personality types.

Re-engineering. Analysing an organisation's structure and processes, and then re-designing the organisation from scratch.

Risk analysis. Part of a method of predicting the amount of risk involved in an endeavour and building contingency for it into the planning phase.

Secondments. A period of time spent working in another role with the assumption that you will return to the original role.

Self managed learning. A learning program designed and undertaken by the individual.

Skills. Expert and practised abilities.

Skills audit route map. A diagram which demonstrates the sequence to take when undertaking a skills audit.

Soft skills. Intangible skills linked to your personality and emotional disposition, for example, assertiveness skills, communication skills, and negotiation skills.

Technical skills. Task performance skills, for example, word processing, driving and computer skills.

Template. A guide for completing a form or document.

Visibility. Level of externally perceived status and esteem.

Workshadowing. Observing another in their work.

Further Reading

Mentoring in Action, David Megginson and David Clutterbuck (Kogan Page).

Get Ahead, Stay Ahead!, Diana Booker (McGraw Hill).

What Colour is Your Parachute?, Richard Nelson Bolles (Ten Speed Press).

Continuous Development, Sue Wood (Institute of Personnel Management).

Developing Attitude Towards Learning, Robert Mager (Kogan Page).

Develop Your Management Potential, John Coopey *et al* (Kogan Page).

Managing Your Own Career, Dave Francis (Collins).

The Career Management Challenge, Peter Herriot (Sage).

Making and Taking Career Changes, John Lynch (British Coal Enterprise).

Play to your Strengths, Tony Buzan (BCA).

The Mind Map Book, Tony Buzan, (BCA).

Some How To Books in this series

Managing Through People, John Humphries.

Managing Your Time, Julie-Ann Amos.

Managing Yourself, Julie-Ann Amos.

Managing Meetings, Ann Dobson.

Investing in People, Dr Harley Turnball.

How To Manage Your Career, Roger Jones.

Surviving Redundancy, Laurel Alexander.

Learning New Job Skills, Laurel Alexander.

Career Networking, Laurel Alexander.

Writing a CV That Works, Paul McGee.

How To Communicate at Work, Ann Dobson.

Maximising Your Memory, Peter Marshall.

Useful Addresses

INSTITUTES AND BUSINESS STUDIES

Institute of Management, Management House, Cottingham Road, Corby, Northants NN17 1TT. Tel: (01536) 204222.

Institute of Personnel Development, IPD House, Camp Road, London SW19 4UX, Tel: (0181) 971 9000.

Chartered Institute of Marketing, Moor Hall, Cookham, Maidenhead, Berks SL6 9QH. Tel: (01628) 427500.

Institute of Administrative Management, 40 Chatsworth Parade, Petts Wood, Orpington, Kent BR5 1RW. Tel: (01689) 875555.

European Association of Professional Secretaries, Patricia Gates, Lovall White Durrant, 65 Holburn Viaduct, London EC1A 2DY. Tel: (0171) 236 0066.

Institute for the Management of Information Systems, IMIS House, Edgington Way, Ruxley, Sidcup, Kent DA14 5HR. Tel: (0181) 308 0747.

Institute of Qualified Private Secretaries, 1st Floor, 6 Bridge Avenue, Maidenhead, Berks SL6 1RR. Tel: (01628) 625007.

Institute of Sales and Marketing Management, Romeland House, Romeland Hill, St Albans, Herts AL3 4ET. Tel: (01727) 812500.

Chamber of Commerce, see your local *Yellow Pages*.

Department of Trade and Industry (DTI). Tel: 0870 1502 500.

The Industrial Society, Peter Runge House, 3 Carlton House, Terrace, London SW1Y 5DG. Tel: (0171) 839 4300.

FLEXIBLE WORKING

New Ways to Work, 309 Upper Street, London N1 2TY. Tel: (0171) 226 4026.

The Industrial Society (as above).

FUNDING

Career Development Loans, FREEPOST, PO Box 99, Sudbury, Suffolk CO10 6BR. Tel: 0800 585505.

TRAINING

Buzan Centres Ltd, 54 Parkstone Road, Poole, Dorset BH15 2PX, (01202) 674676.

Local Colleges, see your local *Yellow Pages*.

Qualfications in Curriculum Authority (*NVQ information*), 22 Euston Road, London NW1 2BZ. Tel: (0171) 728 1893.

Careers Office, see your local *Yellow Pages*.

TRAINING (OPEN LEARNING)

Insight Information, BBC, Broadcasting House, London W1A 1AA.

The Open University, PO Box 71, Milton Keynes, MK1 6AG. Tel: (01908) 274066.

NETWORKING

Women's Business Forum, 191 The Talgarth Road, The Liahuset, Hammersmith, London W6 8BJ. Tel: (0181) 563 8668.

European Women's Management Development Network. Tel: (01256) 767472.

Index

PASSING THAT INTERVIEW
Your step-by-step guide to achieving success

Judith Johnstone

Using a systematic and practical approach, this book takes you step-by-step through the essential pre-interview groundwork, the interview encounter itself, and what you can learn from the experience. The book contains sample pre- and post-interview correspondence, and is complete with a guide to further reading, glossary of terms, and index. 'This is from the first class How To Books stable.' *Escape Committee Newsletter*. 'Offers a fresh approach to a well documented subject.' *Newscheck* (Careers Service Bulletin). 'A complete step-by step guide.' *The Association of Business Executives*. Judith Johnstone is a Member of the Institute of Personnel & Development; she has been an instructor in Business Studies and adult literacy tutor, and has long experience of helping people at work.

144pp illus. 1 85703 360 4. 4th edition.

WRITING A CV THAT WORKS
Developing and using your key marketing tool

Paul McGee

What makes a CV stand out from the crowd? How can you present yourself in the most successful way? This practical book shows you how to develop different versions of your CV for every situation. Reveal your hidden skills, identify your achievements and learn how to communicate these successfully. Different styles and uses for a CV are examined, as you discover the true importance of your most powerful marketing tool. Paul McGee is a freelance Trainer and Consultant for one of Britain's largest out-placement organisations. He conducts marketing workshops for people from all walks of life.

128pp illus. 1 85703 365 5. 2nd edition.

GETTING THAT JOB
The complete job finders handbook

Joan Fletcher

Now in its fourth edition this popular book provides a clear step-by-step guide to identifying job opportunities, writing successful application letters, preparing for interviews and being selected. 'A valuable book.' *Teachers Weekly*. 'Cheerful and appropriate . . . particularly helpful in providing checklists designed to bring system to searching for a job. This relaxed, friendly and very helpful little book could bring lasting benefit.' *Times Educational Supplement*. 'Clear and concise . . . should be mandatory reading by all trainees.' *Comlon Magazine* (LCCI). Joan Fletcher is an experienced Manager and Student Counsellor.

112pp illus. 1 85703 380 9. 4th edition.

IMPROVING YOUR WRITTEN ENGLISH
How to sharpen up your grammar, punctuation and spelling for everyday use

Marion Field

This user-friendly book will be a boon for anyone who needs to brush up his or her English. Written in short, easily understandable sections, it deals with the basics of writing good English. There are sections on punctuation, sentence construction, and spelling. All the common pitfalls are tackled: when to use apostrophes and how to spell those frequently misspelt words. The reader is shown how to adopt the different styles needed for writing a report, essay or short story. Useful exercises and illustrations are included throughout the book. Marion Field has taught English in a variety of secondary schools. For many years she was Head of English in a large Comprehensive School and she is also an examiner for GCSE English.

128pp illus. 1 85703 358 2. 2nd edition.

How To Books provide practical help on a large range of topics. They are available through all good bookshops or can be ordered direct from the distributors. Just tick the titles you want and complete the form on the following page.

___ Achieving Personal Well-being (£8.99)
___ Applying for a Job (£8.99)
___ Arranging Insurance (£9.99)
___ Awakening the Writer Within (£8.99)
___ Backpacking Round Europe (£8.99)
___ Be a Freelance Journalist (£8.99)
___ Be a Freelance Secretary (£8.99)
___ Become a Freelance Sales Agent (£9.99)
___ Becoming a Father (£8.99)
___ Building Self-Esteem (£8.99)
___ Buy & Run a Shop (£8.99)
___ Buy & Run a Small Hotel (£8.99)
___ Buying a Personal Computer (£9.99)
___ Career Networking (£8.99)
___ Career Planning for Women (£8.99)
___ Cash from your Computer (£9.99)
___ Choosing a Nursing Home (£9.99)
___ Choosing a Package Holiday (£8.99)
___ Claim State Benefits (£9.99)
___ Collecting a Debt (£9.99)
___ Communicate at Work (£7.99)
___ Conduct Staff Appraisals (£7.99)
___ Conducting Effective Interviews (£8.99)
___ Controlling Anxiety (£8.99)
___ Coping with Self Assessment (£9.99)
___ Copyright & Law for Writers (£8.99)
___ Creating a Twist in the Tale (£8.99)
___ Creative Writing (£9.99)
___ Critical Thinking for Students (£8.99)
___ Dealing with a Death in the Family (£9.99)
___ Dealing with Your Bank (£8.99)
___ Do Your Own Advertising (£8.99)
___ Do Your Own PR (£8.99)
___ Doing Business Abroad (£10.99)
___ Doing Business on the Internet (£12.99)
___ Doing Voluntary Work Abroad (£9.99)
___ Employ & Manage Staff (£8.99)
___ Find Temporary Work Abroad (£8.99)
___ Finding a Job in Canada (£9.99)
___ Finding a Job in Computers (£8.99)
___ Finding a Job in New Zealand (£9.99)
___ Finding a Job with a Future (£8.99)
___ Finding Work Overseas (£9.99)
___ Freelance DJ-ing (£8.99)
___ Freelance Teaching & Tutoring (£9.99)
___ Get a Job Abroad (£10.99)
___ Get a Job in Europe (£9.99)
___ Get a Job in France (£9.99)
___ Get a Job in Travel & Tourism (£8.99)
___ Get into Radio (£8.99)
___ Getting a Job in America (£10.99)
___ Getting a Job in Australia (£9.99)
___ Getting into Films & Television (£10.99)
___ Getting That Job (£8.99)
___ Getting your First Job (£8.99)
___ Going to University (£8.99)

___ Having a Baby (£8.99)
___ Healing the Hurt Within (£8.99)
___ Helping your Child to Read (£8.99)
___ How to Study & Learn (£8.99)
___ Investing in People (£9.99)
___ Investing in Stocks & Shares (£9.99)
___ Know Your Rights at Work (£8.99)
___ Learning to Counsel (£9.99)
___ Live & Work in Germany (£9.99)
___ Live & Work in Greece (£9.99)
___ Live & Work in Italy (£8.99)
___ Living & Working in America (£12.99)
___ Living & Working in Australia (£12.99)
___ Living & Working in China (£9.99)
___ Living & Working in France (£9.99)
___ Living & Working in Hong Kong (£10.99)
___ Living & Working in New Zealand (£9.99)
___ Living & Working in Spain (£8.99)
___ Living & Working in the Netherlands (£9.99)
___ Living Away From Home (£8.99)
___ Making a Complaint (£8.99)
___ Making a Video (£9.99)
___ Making a Wedding Speech (£8.99)
___ Making Money from Letting (£8.99)
___ Making Money from Writing £8.99)
___ Manage a Sales Team (£8.99)
___ Manage an Office (£8.99)
___ Manage Computers at Work (£8.99)
___ Manage Your Career (£8.99)
___ Managing Budgets & Cash Flows (£9.99)
___ Managing Credit (£8.99)
___ Managing Meetings (£8.99)
___ Managing Projects (£8.99)
___ Managing Through People (£8.99)
___ Managing Your Personal Finances (£8.99)
___ Managing Yourself (£8.99)
___ Market Yourself (£8.99)
___ Mastering Book-Keeping (£8.99)
___ Mastering Business English (£8.99)
___ Mastering Public Speaking (£9.99)
___ Maximising Your Memory (£8.99)
___ Migrating to Canada (£12.99)
___ Obtaining Visas & Work Permits (£9.99)
___ Organising Effective Training (£9.99)
___ Passing Exams Without Anxiety (£8.99)
___ Passing That Interview (£8.99)
___ Plan a Wedding (£8.99)
___ Planning Your Gap Year (£8.99)
___ Preparing a Business Plan (£8.99)
___ Publish a Newsletter (£9.99)
___ Publishing a Book (£9.99)
___ Rent & Buy Property in Italy (£9.99)
___ Research Methods (£8.99)
___ Researching for Writers (£8.99)
___ Retire Abroad (£8.99)
___ Run a Voluntary Group (£8.99)

How To Books

___ Securing a Rewarding Retirement (£8.99)
___ Self-Counselling (£8.99)
___ Selling Your House (£8.99)
___ Setting up Home in Florida (£9.99)
___ Setting Up Your Own Limited Company (£9.99)
___ Spending a Year Abroad (£8.99)
___ Start a Business from Home (£7.99)
___ Start a New Career (£6.99)
___ Starting to Manage (£8.99)
___ Starting to Write (£8.99)
___ Start Word Processing (£8.99)
___ Start Your Own Business (£8.99)
___ Study Abroad (£8.99)
___ Study & Live in Britain (£7.99)
___ Studying at University (£8.99)
___ Studying for a Degree (£8.99)
___ Successful Grandparenting (£8.99)
___ Successful Mail Order Marketing (£9.99)
___ Successful Single Parenting (£8.99)
___ Survive Divorce (£8.99)
___ Surviving Redundancy (£8.99)
___ Taking in Students (£8.99)
___ Taking on Staff (£8.99)
___ Taking Your A-Levels (£8.99)
___ Teach Adults (£8.99)
___ Teaching Abroad (£8.99)
___ Teaching Someone to Drive (£8.99)
___ Thriving on Stress (£8.99)
___ Travel Round the World (£8.99)
___ Unlocking Your Potential (£8.99)
___ Understand Finance at Work (£8.99)
___ Using the Internet (£9.99)

___ Winning Consumer Competitions (£8.99)
___ Winning Presentations (£8.99)
___ Work from Home (£8.99)
___ Work in Retail (£8.99)
___ Working Abroad (£14.99)
___ Working as a Holiday Rep (£9.99)
___ Working as an Au Pair (£8.99)
___ Working in Japan (£10.99)
___ Working in Photography (£8.99)
___ Working in Hotels & Catering (£9.99)
___ Working on Contract Worldwide (£9.99)
___ Working on Cruise Ships (£9.99)
___ Write a Press Release (£9.99)
___ Write & Sell Computer Software (£9.99)
___ Writing a CV that Works (£8.99)
___ Writing a Non Fiction Book (£9.99)
___ Writing a Pantomime (£8.99)
___ Writing a Report (£8.99)
___ Writing a Textbook (£12.99)
___ Writing an Assignment (£8.99)
___ Writing an Essay (£8.99)
___ Writing & Publishing Poetry (£9.99)
___ Writing & Selling a Novel (£8.99)
___ Writing Business Letters (£8.99)
___ Writing for Publication (£9.99)
___ Writing for Radio (£8.99)
___ Writing for Television (£8.99)
___ Writing Humour (£8.99)
___ Writing Reviews (£9.99)
___ Writing Romantic Fiction (£9.99)
___ Writing Science Fiction (£9.99)
___ Writing Short Stories & Articles (£8.99)
___ Writing Your Dissertation (£8.99)

To: Plymbridge Distributors Ltd, Plymbridge House, Estover Road, Plymouth PL6 7PZ. Customer Services Tel: (01752) 202301. Fax: (01752) 202331.

Please send me copies of the titles I have indicated. Please add postage & packing (UK £1, Europe including Eire, £2, World £3 airmail).

☐ I enclose cheque/PO payable to Plymbridge Distributors Ltd for £ _____

☐ Please charge to my ☐ MasterCard, ☐ Visa, ☐ AMEX card.

Account No. ☐☐☐☐☐☐☐☐☐☐☐☐☐☐☐☐

Card Expiry Date ☐☐ 19 ☎ **Credit Card orders may be faxed or phoned.**

Customer Name (CAPITALS) ....

Address ....

.... Postcode ....

Telephone .... Signature ....

Every effort will be made to despatch your copy as soon as possible but to avoid possible disappointment please allow up to 21 days for despatch time (42 days if overseas). Prices and availability are subject to change without notice.

Code BPA